Living the Death of God

Living
the Death
of God

A Theological Memoir

Thomas J. J. Altizer

Foreword by Mark C. Taylor

STATE UNIVERSITY OF NEW YORK PRESS

Published by State University of New York Press, Albany

For information, address State University of New York Press,
194 Washington Avenue, Suite 305, Albany, NY 12210-2384

Production by Judith Block
Marketing by Fran Keneston

Library of Congress Cataloging in Publication Data

Altizer, Thomas J. J.
 Living the death of God : a theological memoir / Thomas J. J. Altizer ; foreword by
Mark C. Taylor.
     p. cm.
 Includes bibliographical references and index.
 ISBN 0-7914-6757-0 (hardcover : alk. paper) — ISBN 0-7914-6758-9 (pbk. : alk.
paper)
 1. Altizer, Thomas J. J. 2. Christian biography. 3. Death of God theology. I. Title.

BX4827.A47A3   2006
230'.092—dc22

2005018665

ISBN-13: 978-0-7914-6757-2 (hardcover : alk. paper)
ISBN-13: 978-0-7914-6758-9 (pbk. : alk. paper)

10 9 8 7 6 5 4 3 2 1

For D. G. Leahy

Contents

Preface

This memoir is a recapitulation of the life work of a radical theologian, intending to recover and renew theological moves occurring over a lifetime, but occurring in the context of an ultimate ending of theology, thereby opening the possibility of the birth of a new and even absolutely new theology. It is to be emphasized that this memoir is not a personal one, but rather a theological memoir, and a memoir intending to record a voyage that is finally a universal one, truly embodied in each of us, whether directly or indirectly, or consciously or unconsciously. Augustine created Western theology by recapitulating such a voyage. This is a voyage that ever more comprehensively has occurred throughout our history, and if that voyage is ending today, its very ending has created a totally new call. That is a calling that is here explored, but explored in the context of our contemporary nihilism, a nihilism here understood to be a reflection of the death of God, yet a death of God that is an actualization of the apocalyptic transfiguration of Godhead itself.

So it is that this memoir is the record of a voyage into an apocalyptic theology, a theology that is our only totally apocalyptic theology, one grounded in a uniquely modern apocalyptic thinking and vision, but no less grounded in a uniquely biblical apocalypse, one never entered by our theological traditions. Inevitably truly new paths must here be sought. If these paths have been forged by great thinkers and visionaries, they have never been mediated to our common life, but a fundamental vocation of theology is to effect such a mediation, and that is attempted in this memoir. Throughout my theological career, I have been accused of writing too abstractly or too abstrusely. Hopefully that can largely be rectified by the genre of the memoir, but nevertheless this writing will be vastly distant from our common theological writing, which is simply closed to the realms explored here. Truly simple theological writing may perhaps be possible for saints, but it was not possible for Augustine, nor for any other truly major theologian, and if it is possible homiletically, that, too, has been central to my theological work. For theology deeply differs from philosophy insofar as it is truly open to proclamation. Thereby it is fully open to all, and is so even in its most radical expressions. I have always been more effective in oral rather than written communication, and this memoir is intended to approximate speech, and to do so not only by way of an intimate address, but by an intimate voice as well.

It was Lissa McCullough who first urged me to write a memoir, and while I initially resisted this, and above all so because of the personal dimension of the memoir, she gradually persuaded me to proceed in my own way, even if this should prove to be a failure. Many have critically responded to this memoir during the years in which it was written, thereby truly strengthening it. These include Mark Taylor, Ray Hart, D. G. Leahy, Lissa McCullough, Brian Schroeder, Yuri Selivanov, Warren Lewis, David Jasper, David Krell, and George Chok. But I am most grateful to Robert Detweiler, who, while in a truly broken condition, gave himself to an extensive critique of the memoir, and virtually all of his suggestions have been incorporated into the text. At one crucial point in the evolution of the memoir, the poet Charles Stein was its editor, the only time that I have been edited by a poet and I also am grateful to another poet and friend, George Quasha, for the title "Living the Death of God." So, too, am I grateful to the State University of New York Press, and particularly to its acquisitions editor, Nancy Ellegate, and grateful again to my superb copyeditor, Lisa Metzger, and to my marvelous production editor, Judith Block. While I have published many books, never before have I had such an overwhelming sense of a writing that is the consequence of a genuine theological community, and while that community includes far more than I can name, it is nonetheless a genuine community, and if only in that community theology is truly alive today.

Foreword:
The Last Theologian

Mark C. Taylor

[I]f all of my genuine theological writing is preaching itself, I can relish an image of myself as a Southern preacher, and perhaps I am the last truly Southern preacher, and if only thereby the last theologian.
—Thomas Jonathan Jackson Altizer

Thomas J. J. Altizer is the last theologian. As such, he is the most God-obsessed person I have ever known. To speak—truly to *speak*—with Altizer is to encounter a passion the excess of which borders on madness. Madness is not a destiny Altizer avoids; to the contrary, he often seems to solicit madness as if it would testify to the truth of his vision. If his mission has a model, it is to be found in the life of his southern ancestor, Stonewall Jackson.

Jackson himself can be understood as having been truly mad, and I have often agonized that insanity is inherent in my family. One uncle murdered his son, another committed suicide, and my father was a deep alcoholic throughout his adult life. Nor was madness alien to our matriarch, who feigned infirmity throughout the time that I knew her, and who ruthlessly dominated her family. None were able truly to rebel against her. This was simply my given world as a child, a world in which the "normal" could only be known as abnormal. Later I could respond to Melville's Captain Ahab as the very soul of America, and an embodiment of its destiny as well.

If the child is the father of the man, then the madness of the Altizer family romance prefigures the madness of his life and work. Altizer *chooses* the fate he suffers, thereby transforming madness into the identity he relentlessly seeks.

This is, of course, no ordinary madness; nor is it literal. The madness that pursues Altizer while he is pursuing it is a holy madness. For those blessed with holy madness, the foolishness of the world can only be overcome by reversing it in a higher madness that negates what others affirm and affirms what others negate. In the following pages, Altizer for the first time discloses the experience, which, he believes, gave rise to his theological vision. Whether this experience was actually as formative as Altizer insists or has grown in importance as it has been filtered through later interpretation, the rudiments of his theology can be discerned in his account. Altizer's narrative inevitably recalls Augustine's experience recounted in his *Confessions.* But whereas Augustine is converted to God, Altizer is converted to Satan.

The decisive event occurred while Altizer was a student in Chicago preparing for a ministerial vocation. The framework he provides for his narrative reveals important dimensions of his lifelong identity. While a seminary student, he was the acting vicar at St. Mark's Church, an interracial Episcopal mission in south Chicago. At the time, candidates for the ministry were required to undergo a thorough psychiatric examination. When the results from the Northwestern Medical School arrived, Altizer unexpectedly discovered that he had "totally failed." Instead of attending the Seabury-Western Seminary for his final year, doctors told him that he "could expect to be in a psychiatric institution within a year." Having provided this background, Altizer proceeds to recount the experience that shaped his life:

> Shortly before this examination, I was in a turbulent condition. While crossing the Midway I would experience violent tremors in the ground, and I was visited by a deep depression, one that had occurred again and again throughout my life, but now with particular intensity. During this period I had perhaps the deepest experience of my life, and one that I believe profoundly affected my vocation as a theologian, and even my theological work itself. This occurred late at night, while I was in my room. I suddenly awoke and became truly possessed, and experienced an epiphany of Satan which I have never been able fully to deny, an

experience in which I could actually feel Satan consuming me, absorbing me into his very being, as though this was the deepest possible initiation and bonding, and the deepest and yet most horrible union. Few who read me know of this experience, but it is not accidental that I am perhaps the only theologian who now writes of Satan, and can jokingly refer to myself as the world's leading Satanologist; indeed, Satan and Christ soon became my primary theological motifs, and my deepest theological goal eventually became one of discovering a *coincidentia oppositorum* between them.

Throughout his entire theological career, Altizer *never* loses sight of this goal. Indeed, his entire theological project is an extended meditation on the radical implications of the *coincidential oppositorum* of Christ and Satan. This coincidence of opposites informs Altizer's thinking and transforms the passion that shapes his lifeinto what can only be understood as the *imitatio Christi*.

One of the most impressive things about Altizer's theological corpus is its utter consistency. Few thinkers in the history of theology or philosophy have pursued their fundamental insight with such tenacity and rigor. For Altizer, the deepest religious and theological truths are always "genuinely paradoxical." In attempting to fathom the implications of the *coincidentia oppositorum* lying at the heart of theological truth, he relentlessly struggles to comprehend without unraveling the "absolute paradox" of Christian life. This paradox, Altizer believes, can only be grasped by a thinking that is thoroughly dialectical. Though he traces the roots of this dialectical theology back through Luther and Augustine to Paul, the thinkers that most decisively shape Altizer's work are modern. Indeed, the truth embodied in Jesus and disclosed to Altizer in his shattering experience cannot become fully manifest until the modern era. "If a *coincidentia oppositorum* between Christ and Satan is a deep center of the Christian epic, it only gradually evolves or becomes manifest, not being fully called forth until modernity, and only full modernity has envisioned the totality of Hell, or the absolute abyss or total darkness, a vision of the ultimate and final depths of an absolutely alien abyss that can be discovered in every primal expression of the late modern imagination." When the coincidence of opposites is grasped dialectically, it becomes clear that affirmation and negation are inseparable. Altizer

discovers this interplay of affirmation and negation in the writings of
the three figures who have most influenced his thinking: Blake, Hegel,
and Nietzsche. These pivotal thinkers, he maintains, develop different
variations of the same fundamental insight: every Yes harbors a No,
and every No is at the same time a Yes. When Yes is No, and No is
Yes, the sacred is the profane, and the profane is sacred. Repeating
Hegel's insight, Altizer argues that modernity realizes the truth Jesus
initially proclaimed.

It is important to understand that the "coincidence" of opposites is
not the "union" of opposites. When opposites coincide, they are not
reconciled but juxtaposed to create a tension, which is simultaneously
the most profound suffering and its overcoming. As Altizer's thinking
matures, he comes to understand this passion in terms of the death of
God. Far from an abstract philosophical concept or literary trope, the
death of God is, for Altizer, an actual historical event first enacted in
the person of Jesus and then actualized in the course of history, which
culminates in the "absolute abyss or total darkness" of modernity. This
darkness is the result of the disappearance of everything once known
as God. In the absence of God, an incomprehensible void overwhelms
human existence. But darkness, like everything else, is both itself and
its opposite. Thus, for those with eyes to see, utter darkness is at the
same time pure light. While repeatedly stressing the uniqueness of
modernity and the radicality of his theological interpretation of it,
Altizer also acknowledges his agreement with what he describes as
"classical theology." For the Christian, there can be no redemption
without damnation. When sin is accepted, the No of damnation is
transformed into the Yes of redemption. This dialectical reversal of
negation into affirmation is not merely the function of subjective experience but signals an actual "transfiguration of Godhead itself."

Yet is this actually possible? Is it even possible to understand any kind
of transfiguration of the Godhead, or does this occur in Luther's understanding of justification itself, a justification ultimately demanding a
transfiguration of the God of judgment into the God of grace, and is
that understanding already present in Paul, and one which has been a
deep underground of Christianity throughout its history? Certainly it is
not possible to think such a transfiguration apart from defying the deep-

est theological authority. This occurs in both Paul and Luther, of course, but must it occur in every genuine theological thinking?

In saying Yes to Jesus, one *affirms* both the No of sin and the Yes of salvation, thereby accepting one's paradoxical condition as *simul iustus et peccator*. This paradox is, in Kierkegaard's terms, absolute because it cannot be overcome through the machinations of reason. And yet, Altizer's dialectical vision is as Hegelian as it is Kierkegaardian. By saying Yes to both the No of damnation and the Yes of redemption, he negates negation. This double negation is an absolute affirmation, which embraces the fallen world in such a way that it becomes the Kingdom of God.

It is precisely the absolute paradox of double negation, incarnate in the life and death of Jesus, that Altizer, again following Kierkegaard, believes Christendom negates. For Kierkegaard, as for Nietzsche, the church consistently denies what Jesus had affirmed. The only way to recover the truth of Christian revelation, therefore, is to negate Christendom. If this negation is not to repeat the error it seeks to overcome, it must not be a simple negation, which is a mere rejection; to the contrary, the radical Christian *affirms* the *negation* of Christendom. This affirmation of negation does not involve the mere recollection of or return to the past, but brings about radical novelty by creating a condition that has never before existed. The repetition of the Absolute Paradox extends the dialectic of crucifixion and resurrection to nature (i.e., space) and history (i.e., time). The culmination of this incarnational process is the "full and total *coincidentia oppositorum* of the sacred and the profane," which occurs for the first time in the modern world. For modernity, the sacred is profane and the profane is sacred. Just as crucifixion harbors resurrection, so the disappearance of God turns out to be God's final revelation. In the modern or late modern world, God is *totally present as absent*; or, conversely, *absence is the presence of God*.

This insight can be expressed in terms that suggest important similarities between Christianity and certain versions of Buddhism. From his first book, *Oriental Mysticism and Biblical Eschatology*, Altizer has insisted that at the deepest level Christianity and Buddhism share fundamental beliefs. Most important, for the Buddhist, as for the

radical Christian, reality is absolute nothingness, and absolute nothingness is absolutely real. The Christian can embrace this terrifying
truth in the "absolute darkness" of the modern world where God is
"totally absent": "Finally, this is a darkness in response to which we
can only say Yes, and if this is our deeper theological calling, one to
which everyone is called, my way has been one of naming that darkness as God. While I believe that ultimately we can only say Yes to
God, now that means saying Yes to the absolute darkness or the
absolute nothingness of God, and hence saying Yes to absolute nothingness or absolute darkness itself." To say Yes to this absolute nothingness is to discover plenitude in the void. This fullness in no way
represses or forgets the emptiness in the midst of life but allows us to
live with an abandon that embraces loss and lack as the very condi-
tions of our existence.

In modernity, it is writers and artists rather than theologians who
teach this difficult truth. While following Hegel at every turn, Altizer
sometimes finds it necessary to reverse the Hegelian dialectic to make
his point. While Hegel translates artistic images and theological repre-
sentations into philosophical concepts, Altizer translates philosophical
concepts into artistic images and theological rhetoric. From the writings of Kafka and Beckett to paintings of Van Gogh and Monet,
Altizer repeatedly rediscovers the God who is not namable as God in
works of art. For those who can see in the dark, the Unnamable is the
name of God today.

For Altizer, the question of style is a matter of substance. Always
the Southern preacher, his sentences are crafted to be spoken rather
than read. He defiantly rejects the protocols of academic writing,
which, he believes, destroy the passion that is the pulse of insight. The
absence of footnotes and dearth of citations testify to a longing for
originality that lies at the heart of modernism. Listening to the cadence
and rhythm of his texts, sentences whose length and complexity on the
printed page baffle more than communicate assume a coherence that
makes them rhetorically effective. Altizer believes in the power of the
word as much as his great Protestant precursors. The Word is not only
epistemological but ontological; its effects are a matter of being as
well as knowing. Since words change things, speech can actually be
redemptive. When "truly actual speech" is apprehended in "true hear-

ing," reality itself is transformed. Speech extends the incarnational process by providing the occasion for an experience as passionate as that suffered by Jesus and undergone by Altizer. When poetic speech is effective, the Word becomes incarnate in the life of the person who receives it. In this way, the words of the theologian become the vehicle for redemptive transformation.

But words are not always effective. A profound sense of failure pervades Altizer's *Theological Memoir*. This failure extends beyond academic positions never offered and readers' lack of understanding. The failure haunting Altizer is more serious and more interesting. As his reflections draw to a close, he admits that he fears having betrayed his own theological vision.

> I deeply believe that each and every one of us is called to a theological voyage, and that it inevitably occurs whether or not we are aware of it, so that in this sense theology is our most universal way, and even if theology has never been so invisible as it is today, that invisibility could be a necessary mask for its contemporary actuality, and my gravest fear about my own work is that it is an irresponsible dislodging of that mask, and one only unveiling a hollow and artificial theology. Perhaps any such unveiling will inevitably suffer this consequence, or any unveiling of our lesser voyages, but even those voyages challenge that deep silence that reigns among us, and while many can know silence as a deep theological virtue, it can no less so be an ultimate theological veil and curse.

Obsessed with God, Altizer is compelled to rend the veil of God's invisibility. By naming the unnamable "God," he attempts to reveal divine presence in absence.

> One might think of a canary in the mine when considering my theological life: so long as there is any movement at all the darkness is not yet total. But this is a darkness in which genuine mining is occurring, and even if it is unheard and invisible to us, if we can name our darkness we can remain open to that mining, and this naming could be understood as the purest vocation of theology. Yes, the primary calling of the theologian is to name God, and to name that God who can actually be named by us, and if this calling has seemingly now ended, that could be

because the theologian has not yet truly named our darkness, and thus not yet truly named God. While silence is now the primary path of the theologian, and above all silence about God, this is a silence which I have ever more deeply and ever more comprehensively refused, for I am simply incapable of not naming God, and perhaps most deeply because of that very initiation which I was given.

Altizer is incapable of not naming God because he longs for a rebirth of theology. In matters theological as well as personal, he simply cannot imagine a death that is not a resurrection. This longing for a rebirth of theology, however, betrays Altizer's theological vision. His work provides an eloquent testimony to the *impossibility* of theology in a postmodern world. Theology ends with the death of God. Appearances to the contrary notwithstanding, the continuing chatter across the theological spectrum is a symptom of the exhaustion of theology. To remain true to Altizer's extraordinary theological vision, it is necessary to guard the silence he cannot avoid breaking. In this sacred silence, the unsettling words of the last theologian will continue to echo forever.

CHAPTER 1

The Calling

This memoir is intended to be a voyage returning to those moments and grounds which occasioned and made possible my theological vocation, a vocation inseparable from everything that I have known as destiny. Hence it is not the consequence of a free choice in the common sense, but is inescapably my destiny, and while I have chosen it again and again, I look upon such choice simply as an acceptance of that which I have most deeply been given. Never have I known a moment truly free of this vocation, nor have I ever been truly tempted to abandon it; it is as though it is simply an irrevocable given, one simply unchallengeable, for it is deeper than anything else which I can know, even if it ever remains a mystery to me. This is the mystery that I shall attempt to explore in this memoir, and to do so by seeking to unravel its history, or its history in what little I can remember, and just as memory itself is a deep mystery, it is nonetheless inescapable. It is certainly inescapable here.

I was born into a family that at bottom is deeply Southern, although my mother was a southerner only by adoption, and we were West Virginians, and thus border people. My family sense was most determined by my descent from Stonewall Jackson on my father's mother side, for the origins of my grandfather on my father's side were deeply hidden, and my late discovery of this origin came as an ultimate shock. The dominant figure in our family was my father's mother, who was a true Southern matriarch. She had been widowed in early middle age, after having borne four sons. Her husband was a self-made man, and not only self-made but self-taught, who had become a lawyer through his own power, and a quite successful one, being one of the founders of West Virginia's natural gas company, and a major attorney in Charleston, West Virginia. I lived for most of my childhood and adolescence in my grandmother's large and magnificent house. Servants were my primary source of care and guidance, but I was truly ashamed of this luxurious site, and already in early childhood knew a deep loneliness. I was taught to "walk tall," and to distance myself from everything that is "common," a role imposing its own solitude, and I have known solitude throughout my life.

Above all I was immersed in images of Stonewall, again and again given the sense that his destiny was now my own, and while I knew little then of Stonewall's ultimate Calvinism, I have come to recognize that my ever fuller commitment to predestination is a consequence of my Jackson heritage. Jackson himself can be understood as having been truly mad, and I have often agonized that insanity is inherent in my family. One uncle murdered his son, another committed suicide, and my father was a deep alcoholic throughout his adult life. Nor was madness alien to our matriarch, who feigned infirmity throughout the time that I knew her, and who ruthlessly dominated her family. None were able truly to rebel against her. This was simply my given world as a child, a world in which the "normal" could only be known as abnormal. Later I could respond to Melville's Captain Ahab as the very soul of America, and an embodiment of its destiny as well. However, I did grow up in a house in which books were sacred, a house dominated by a very large and marvelous library. Reading has always been my primary vocation and avocation, and my father was here my major guide, for he had fully intended to be a professor of literature until his mother refused this path. Indeed, his father had been a genuine lover of books, who had only once violated them—when he hurled Nietzsche's *The Antichrist* into the fireplace (a premonition of the destiny of his grandson?).

I never knew this patriarch, called Tizer by his friends, and we were forbidden to inquire into his origins, which in a Southern context is inexplicable. These origins were deeply Southern, for as I eventually discovered, the Altizer clan of southwestern Virginia (and all Altizers descend from it), was dominated by a terror of miscegenation, hence they were forbidden to marry outside the clan, and when I visited their graveyard, in a vast and beautiful and abandoned area now said to be cursed, I discovered that Altizer is the only name among its tombstones. Madness? Yes, but not an uncommon one in the South, and if all deep history is forbidden, surely ours was, except for the commanding figure of Stonewall Jackson, who vicariously gave me my name, Thomas Jonathan Jackson.

At the height of the death of God controversy, while I was on a speaking tour of Virginia colleges, I formally addressed the Virginia Military Institute, which continues to regard Stonewall as its true founder. My address was given at a solemn occasion in the institute's chapel, one dominated by an icon of Stonewall. I had been introduced by the Commandant of VMI as the first descendant of Stonewall to speak here, and this occurred only after I had been escorted by VMI's chaplain to the grave of Stonewall, where I had laid myself above his bones and prayed for his spirit to inspire me. Now before this solemn assembly, all in full dress uniform, and accompanied by their military band, I proclaimed the death of God in the name of Stonewall. Not a sound could then be heard, and the program ended as though nothing untoward had occurred. It was followed by a party lasting almost until dawn, and I sensed that this was, indeed, a genuine celebration of Stonewall. For it has been my experience that the death of God resonates far more deeply in the South than elsewhere in the country, perhaps because the South has been so obsessed with God, and unlike New England where Puritanism is little more than a distant memory, an American Calvinism continues to reign in the South, or did throughout my experience of it, and if this is manifest in a uniquely Southern literature, it is no less manifest in a genuinely Southern theology. Here, once again, I accepted my destiny.

Although my home was little more than nominally Christian, I was obsessed with Christianity throughout my youth, assembling my own little chapel where I fervently prayed. I had no real religious guidance at all, being forced thereby to find my own way. This has continued throughout my life, except insofar as I came under the influence of religious masters—primarily through reading—and when I did attempt both a monastic and a ministerial vocation, I simply failed. While a theological student, I was chaplain or acting vicar of an interracial Episcopal mission in south Chicago, St. Mark's Church, at that time the only such mission in the Episcopal Diocese of Chicago. We were virtually ignored by all church authorities, except for my guiding pastor, Robert Reister, but this was an exciting experience for me, both in its pastoral and in its preaching responsibilities, and I was persuaded that I had a genuine vocation for the ministry. But the time came for me to be given a psychiatric examination as a prerequisite for my candidacy for the priesthood of the Episcopal Church. I unexpectedly and totally failed. This examination had been conducted at the Northwestern Medical School, given by a professor of psychiatry who had published a huge tome on psychological testing, which I was informed by his associates was the most authoritative in its field. A variety of tests and interviews had resulted in the judgment that I was truly mentally ill, or so I was informed by the dean of the Seabury-Western Seminary where I was expected to spend a final year of theological study in preparation for ordination, and I was seriously advised that I could expect to be in a psychiatric institution within a year. At last I received scientific confirmation of my madness, and while this came as a terrible shock, my beloved professor, Joachim Wach, insisted that it was an act of both providence and grace, for if I had no true vocation for the ministry, I did have one for theology, and that could most effectively be conducted outside the church.

Shortly before this examination, I was in a turbulent condition. While crossing the Midway I would experience violent tremors in the ground, and I was visited by a deep depression, one that had occurred again and again throughout my life, but now with particular intensity. During this period I had perhaps the most ultimate experience of my life, and one that I believe profoundly affected my vocation as a theologian, and even my theological work itself. This occurred late at night, while I was in my room. I suddenly awoke and became truly possessed, and experienced an epiphany of Satan which I have never been able fully to deny, an experience in which I could actually feel Satan consuming me, absorbing me into his very being, as though this was the deepest possible initiation and bonding, and the deepest and yet most horrible union. Few who read me know of this experience, but it is not accidental that I am perhaps the only theologian who now writes of Satan, and can jokingly refer to myself as the world's leading Satanologist; indeed, Satan and Christ soon became my primary theological motifs, and my deepest theological goal eventually became one of discovering a *coincidentia oppositorum* between them.

Nevertheless, it cannot be denied that failing the examination was a profoundly traumatic experience for me. I certainly was very close to a genuine perishing, and the one who most effectively brought hope and succor to me in that crisis was Wilber Katz, former dean of the University of Chicago Law School, who as a deeply committed Episcopalian had been my ally and primary guide at St. Mark's. Wilber offered to pay for my psychoanalysis, and when I refused this, he himself gave me genuine and extended therapy. I continue to believe that he was a pastor in the truest sense. While I was a student at the University of Chicago (1947–1954), I experienced solitude and genuine friendship simultaneously, and this has largely been true throughout my life. As a theological student I was then perhaps unique, rebelling against the Chicago liberal theological tradition, being forced to teach myself Kierkegaard and Barth, and in desperation moving from the theological field to the history of religions, where I discovered a genuine community, which we always referred to as the Sangha. During this period the University of Chicago had eliminated the credit system, and advancement was solely by way of examination. While this brought with it a genuine freedom for the student, it had disastrous effects if one attempted to transfer to another institution. In my case it would have meant the loss of three years of study, which I simply could not afford. While I never became a genuine historian of religions, I did employ the history of religions as a way into a new form of theology. This was fully accepted by Wach and the Sangha, but not, I fear, by the theological faculty. Indeed, when I was recommended for a fellowship in the history of religions, this was refused by the governing faculty committee on the grounds that I was disloyal to the Divinity School (yes, this was the McCarthy era), and even when I was the first to complete the history of religions doctoral exam with distinction, this was never recorded in my university record. It is as though I was invisible as a Divinity School student, but I have come to pride myself on being their most disloyal alumnus, even if as a radical theologian I am a rebirth of the early Chicago theological tradition, a tradition always hidden from us. The most distinguished Chicago theologian is Henry Nelson Wieman, and he did have an impact in my day, but not as a radical theologian, which he certainly was, but rather as a process or dipolar theologian, even if this is alien to Wieman's real work. Only very gradually was I able to discover the radical religious and theological tradition of America. American historians, with the exception of Perry Miller, have done an excellent job in disguising this, but this is a tradition with which I have come to identify, even if its deepest American ground is alien to me, a ground resurrected in the revolutionary work of D. G. Leahy.

My deepest theological conflict in my Chicago days was between my Protestant and my Catholic poles, one originally given me by the Episcopal Church, and soon I became ravaged by what Anglicans call "Roman fever." I attended or attempted to attend mass daily, was instructed by the university Catholic chaplain, read voluminously in Catholic literature—my primary Catholic master being John Henry Newman—and was deeply frustrated by the impossibility then of studying Catholicism at the University of Chicago. Yet one of my professors, Coert Rylaarsdam, spent long sessions with me, guiding me into a Catholic-Protestant union or synthesis, to which he was committed, even urging me to become a Jesuit so that I could prosecute this vocation, but I soon realized in these days prior to the Second Vatican Council that it was impossible to be a Catholic theologian in America, and Walter Ong informed me that the Society of Jesus here deterred its most brilliant members from becoming theologians because genuinely creative theological work was forbidden. Of course, it was soon forbidden in Protestantism just as it was becoming possible in Catholicism, and if there is now no real Catholic-Protestant theological dialogue, this is because we are now largely bereft of Protestant theologians, for as Tillich foresaw, Protestantism can survive only as the Protestant principle, a principle even now being incorporated within Catholicism.

This was the conflict that was the driving force in my master's thesis, "Nature and Grace in the Theology of Augustine," a thesis initiated by my persuasion that the deepest division or dichotomy between Catholicism and Protestantism derives from their profoundly opposing conceptions of nature and grace, and just as Augustine is the deepest theological influence upon both Catholicism and Protestantism, it is at this very point that his influence is most dichotomous. My thesis was that the primal relationship between nature and grace is the true center of Augustine's theology, one which the Catholic understands as a polar relationship and the Protestant understands as a dichotomous relationship. Both Protestantism and Catholicism are genuinely Augustinian at this crucial point, for Augustine, as witness his Neoplatonic and his Pauline poles, was truly ambivalent or paradoxical in his thinking here. Yet if this ambivalence could be resolved, then here lies a way to a genuine coinherence if not union between Catholicism and Protestantism. Yet I also looked upon Augustine as the theological source of modernity itself, for I was already, even if only unconsciously, embarked upon my project of correlating Augustine and Nietzsche. I was immersed in Nietzsche while writing this thesis, and just as my later work explores the deeply Augustinian ground of Nietzsche's thinking, my earliest theological work explored Augustine within a Nietzschean perspective. My thesis was deeply affected by my conviction that it was Augustine who philosophically and theologically discovered the subject or the center of consciousness, and it was Nietzsche who first fully or decisively discovered the dissolution of that subject, and if only here philosophical and theological thinking are truly united.

The truth is that I was unable to resolve or even truly conclude my master's thesis. Perhaps this is simply impossible, but that very blockage was a deep turning point for me, and I became convinced that I simply could not work within our existing theological traditions. Hence I had a real theological reason for entering the study of the history of religions, and I became persuaded that a new theological ground could be discovered by way of a voyage to the East. While this is seemingly a commonplace in full modernity, no theologian had chosen this path, and even today we are virtually bereft of genuine East-West theologies; or, insofar as they exist, they have come from the East and not the West, and at no other point is there a greater rift between the rhetoric of our theological discourse and its actual accomplishments. Of course, I was a rank amateur in the history of religions—I never learned the languages that I should have, though Wach tolerated this because he knew who I am—but I did make a serious attempt to understand Mahayana Buddhist philosophy, and while this was wholly for a theological purpose, I continue to believe that this is a genuine route into a truly new theology.

I did not meet Mircea Eliade until after I had left Chicago, but our initial encounter was a deep one for me. I shall never forget how he described to me what he intended to be his magnum opus, a comprehensive work ranging through the deepest expressions of both literature and religion, and seeking to demonstrate in their highest and purest expressions a full and pure *coincidentia oppositorum* of the sacred and profane. No one whom I have known has influenced me more deeply than Eliade; certainly I owe him an incalculable debt, but perhaps his deepest gift was his very support: No one else has encouraged me more deeply, or opened more vistas to be discovered, vistas inseparable from a truly new theology; Eliade knew the deep necessity of such a theology, and knew it as has no theologian. Indeed, Eliade has a unique understanding of the radical profane, one he could realize by way of his very knowledge of the pure or radical sacred, for Eliade's is a dialectical understanding, and one most deeply grounded in an ultimate *coincidentia oppositorum*. Moreover, Eliade envisions a primordial eclipse or death of God, one occurring by way of the eclipse of the primordial sky god and the consequent advent of what we know as religion, which in this perspective is itself the consequence of a primordial fall. So, too, Eliade, as an Eastern Christian, could know a uniquely modern death of God as having its origin in the very advent of Western Christianity, but this advent itself is a repetition of the primordial death of God, and an advent that will finally culminate in a *coincidentia oppositorum* between the sacred and the profane.

Clearly such a *coincidentia oppositorum* is a deep ground of all my work, so if only at this point I am a genuine Eliadean, and initially my real theological voyage was made possible by an opening to the truly sacred ground of the radical profane. Hence I was ever more fully drawn into Nietzsche, the purest thinker of the radical profane, and this most decisively occurred while I was teaching at Wabash College. Moreover, in June of 1955, while reading Erich Heller's essay on Nietzsche and Rilke for the seventh time in a library at the University of Chicago, I had what I have ever since regarded as a genuine religious conversion, and this was a conversion to the death of God. For then I truly experienced the death of God, and experienced it as a conversion, and thus as the act and grace of God himself. Never can such an experience be forgotten, and while it truly paralleled my earlier experience of the epiphany of Satan, this time I experienced a pure grace, as though it were the very reversal of my experience of Satan.

But now I knew that "Satan" is dead, and has died for me. The identification of God and Satan is Blake's most revolutionary vision, but at that time I had only begun an exploration of Blake, and had no explicit awareness of any such identification, so that I could not then name that God who is dead as Satan. But I could know God as the God who is truly dead, and at bottom I knew that this was a genuine theological understanding of God, and one demanding a transformation of theology itself. Then I was impelled to begin the process of reversing my deepest theological roots, and this initially occurred by way of a reversal of that Barthianism which I had so deeply absorbed. This took place over many months when I returned to Indiana, spending most of my evenings intensively thinking about Barth while drinking bourbon and listening to the original recording of *The Threepenny Opera*. Somehow I was purged, or think that I was, for there are those who continue to identify me as a Barthian, and it is true that Barth is the only modern theologian whom I profoundly respect.

All of this lies beneath the writing of my first book, *Oriental Mysticism and Biblical Eschatology*, yet this was only the first step in my new theological voyage, and while the book truly embarrasses me now, I am most distressed that its all too faulty execution hides and obscures its real intention, and to this day it is the only book on this extraordinarily important subject. It was written while I was teaching at Emory University in Atlanta, where I came under the impact of Walter Strauss, Gregor Sebba, and John Cobb, and also under the impact of the New Testament scholars William Beardslee, James Robinson, Robert Funk, Norman Perrin, and Hendrik Boers, all of whom became progressively radical while at Emory. It was as though Emory was a truly radical center, or surely it was so theologically. Such an environment would be impossible to imagine today, but that was a time of breakthrough theologically, and above all so in America, that new America which at that very time was becoming the dominant power in the world. If America was now the new Rome, we sensed that a deep destiny had been thrust upon us. Most concretely, theology had to be liberated from its deeply European theological ground, and this surely occurred in a uniquely American Bultmannianism, one dissolving if not reversing the neo-orthodox ground of modern European theology. Emory was the center of this radical Bultmannianism, for at this time it was New Testament scholars who were our most radical theologians, and while certainly the work of Bultmann himself and his German followers was a fundamental ground of this movement, it was in America that this radical hermeneutics became most open and decisive, and it had a profound impact upon me. Of course, modern biblical scholarship has always been an ultimate threat to theology, ever more fully unearthing a vast distance between theological language and its biblical ground, but not until the Second World War, when Bultmannian demythologizing was born, did this distance become fully manifest. Bultmann and his European followers could not break from a neo-orthodox theological ground, this first occurred in America, and ironically most fully occurred at the very center of the Bible Belt.

Demythologizing was most deeply directed at an original Christian apocalypticism, one that continues to this very day; it is a historical recognition of that apocalypticism which impels demythologizing, one which is perhaps deepest in our new apocalyptic world. Then theological upheaval inevitably occurs, one from which my work is inseparable, but in the 1960s this seemed to be occurring universally, and apparently occurring in a new and universal apocalypticism. This was a time when American radicals could identify America itself as Satanic, Satanic in its imperialism, its capitalism, its racism, its demonic war in Vietnam; yet America was nevertheless vibrantly alive, and most alive in its very radicalism, which then pervaded not only all of the arts, but theology itself, which helped to drive older radical theologians such as Reinhold Niebuhr and Paul Tillich to a new conservatism. I could rejoice when Tillich later declared to me that the real Tillich is the radical Tillich, but at that time the theological battle was most openly and perhaps most deeply waged in the Catholic world; Catholic conservatives could identify both Teilhard and Rahner as Satanic, but in the sixties Catholic and Protestant radicals were united. We still lack a study of theological radicalism in the sixties. Few are aware of how pervasive it was, and if I had to cite a book which most purely embodies it, that book could only be Norman O. Brown's *Love's Body*.

Upon the completion of *Oriental Mysticism and Biblical Eschatology*, I recognized that I had to return to Eliade, and to do so by writing an Eliadean theological book, a book whose original title was "The Dialectic of the Sacred," ultimately published as *Mircea Eliade and the*

Dialectic of the Sacred. It was intended to lay the groundwork for a theological *coincidentia oppositorum*. This book, too, was under the impact of my Emory friends and associates, and most so in its literary interpretations; literature and theology was then a promising new field, and while it has come to little in the theological world, it is richly present in literary studies, as I fully discovered when I later embarked upon a study of the Christian epic. Yet for the first time Nietzsche was the very center of my theological thinking, and what is most radical in this book is its identification of Nietzsche's vision of Eternal Recurrence as a genuine renewal and resurrection of a uniquely biblical Kingdom of God. It is just thereby a *coincidentia oppositorum* of the radical sacred and the radical profane, thereby renewing in a radically profane world that Kingdom of God which Jesus enacted and proclaimed, and most clearly so in that total and apocalyptic Yes which is here enacted. This is the book which most openly establishes the foundations of my theological work, and ever since I have been persuaded that Nietzsche is our purest uniquely modern theologian, and even our purest theologian since Augustine himself.

Despite the fact that I had published two books and many articles, I still had not become a genuine writer. This, I believe, occurred with the writing of my third book, *The New Apocalypse: The Radical Christian Vision of William Blake*. I wrote it while on sabbatical in Chicago, where I established a deep relationship with Eliade, which continued until his death. I participated in the Tillich-Eliade seminar on theology and the history of religions, and was able to conduct a genuine theological dialogue with Tillich himself. This was the time of a comprehensive theological breakthrough for me. I was working upon the most radical of all Christian visionaries, discovering an inspiration which I had never known before, attempting to identify myself with Blake, and finding that a total reversal of all Christian imagery and symbolism is the very way to its resurrection for us, a resurrection which has already occurred, and is even now our most ultimate ground. It is not insignificant that theology has so resisted our profoundest visionaries. All of them have been truly and comprehensively heterodox, only here can we discover the deepest heresy, and discover it in the very depth of such vision. Certainly there is every reason for condemning Blake, but if he is the true inaugurator of a uniquely modern imaginative world, he is just thereby the inaugurator of a truly

new religious or sacred world, and a new world or new apocalypse
that is simultaneously Christian and universal at once.

At first I could find no publisher for my Blake manuscript, and in
returning to Emory I was caught up in a new theological fervor which
was beginning to grip the country. This occasioned my writing of *The
Gospel of Christian Atheism*, which immediately became a theological
scandal, perhaps simply because of its title, for there is little evidence
that more than a few have actually read the book. And so far as I
know, for the first time a book was published with a deeply negative
criticism included on its very jacket. Yet I admired its publisher, the
Westminster Press, which was then a major theological publisher, and
it surely took courage for them to publish this book. A storm had
broken out even before it was published, initiated by the *New York
Times* and *Time* magazine. Their articles on the new death of God theology were remarkably responsible: a *Time* editor called me to check
with me exactly what they said about my theology, and despite its necessary brevity I could only concur. The truth is that journalists read the
new theology more responsibly than did many, if not most, theologians, and for two years radical theology was at the forefront of the
mass media; it was as though the country itself was possessed by a
theological fever, and a radical theological fever, one in which the
most religious nation in the industrial world had suddenly discovered
its own deep atheism, and while it was accidental that this should
focus upon a few theologians, it is not accidental that such a discovery
occurred, or that it has subsequently passed into a mass amnesia.

Throughout this period my deepest comrade was William Hamilton. We had corresponded for many years, but only fully came to
know each other when he invited me to visit his theological seminary,
Colgate-Rochester in New York, where he was under deep attack. We
then formed an alliance, which subsequently resulted in the publication of several of our articles under the title *Radical Theology and the
Death of God*. While we are very different theologically, we also share
many common motifs, and it was Bill who most effectively goaded me
in the direction of a fully kenotic or self-emptying theology; but Bill is
a genuine pastor, as I am not, and also one who has mastered more
than any other theologian the new world of the mass media, having
created and conducted a national CBS weekly television series on the
death of God, and doubtless this was a major factor evoking the theo-

logical scandal which occurred soon after this. The scandal revolved around the public furor caused by theologians embracing the death of God and doing so in the name of faith itself. Frankly, both Bill and I are preachers, but I am a Southern preacher, as he is not; we often appeared together publicly, each speaking as preachers, and each evoking both positive and deeply negative responses. I sensed that I could be hated much more than Bill, indeed hated more purely than any other theologian, but Bill could often win us acceptance, and he surely could write for the public as I could not. Yet I was much more deeply supported by friends and colleagues than was Bill, as witness the response of our respective institutions: Bill was no longer allowed to teach theology, while Emory fully supported me in this time of crisis, and did so under intense public and private fire. Legally, Emory is a Methodist institution, and the Southern Board of Methodist Bishops publicly demanded my immediate dismissal, just as a great many alumni and supporters of Emory publicly declared that they would cease all support of their university if I were not fired forthwith.

However, it is also true that when the president of Emory, Sanford Atwood, refused to dismiss me, and this was reported on the front page of *The New York Times,* the Ford Foundation immediately sent some of their executives to Emory to assist it, whereas previously Emory had almost always failed in its Ford Foundation applications. Administrative calculations later reached the judgment that Emory had lost and gained about an equal amount because of the scandal; still later their alumni magazine published a long article on the affair which advanced the thesis that the scandal had made Emory into a national institution. Be that as it may, theology then enjoyed national and even world attention which is inconceivable today. Books and innumerable articles appeared about American radical theology throughout the world, dozens if not hundreds of theses and dissertations were written about the death of God theology, symposiums on it seemed to be occurring everywhere, and our books were translated into many languages.

CHAPTER 2

New York

When John Cobb and Jim Robinson accepted an invitation to play a decisive role in establishing a new graduate theological center in California, I was deeply tempted to join them. We had intimately worked together in planning a new religious studies graduate program at Emory, and were committed to a truly new theology. The only opening then at Claremont, however, was a professorship of homiletics, and while I was willing to accept it, their dean wisely refused. Despite my alienation from the church, I was and am deeply committed to preaching, but we overwhelmingly need a truly new preaching. As Bob Funk, a former boy evangelist himself, continually remarked, the gospel has been literally repeated so many times that it has lost all of its original or fundamental meaning. Hence it has become what Nietzsche identified as *dysangel*, a reversal of the original gospel, and nowhere more so than in America. I first became aware of the rumbling that was to become the death of God controversy while visiting to give a lecture at the Episcopal Seminary of the Southwest. The professor of homiletics there initiated me into the new world of preaching and the mass media, and sensing what was about to happen to me, he gave me excellent advice about how to respond to the mass media. The practical wisdom that I then learned, and practiced ever more fully as time went on, was how to respond to questions of a television interviewer. The trick is to look the camera fully in the eye while answering the question, but to ignore the question itself altogether in responding. For this makes possible speaking what one intends, and I knew that I intended to preach in that situation.

Already Kierkegaard had taught me that true preaching is inevitably a profound offense. It is precisely that which most deeply offends which is authentic preaching, so the "good news" of the gospel can only be heard by us as "bad news." It is a reversal of everything that is immediately our own, of everything that is actuality for us. Once the death of God controversy fully broke, I was continually on television. As I traveled about the country, I was invariably interviewed for local television, and I always responded with preaching; perhaps I was the first television evangelist, and I preached by declaring that everything we know as God is dead, and that this death is the gospel, is the "good news," I would pronounce this with as much passion as possible, and proclaim it as the full and final advent of an absolute joy. What I intended was to seek out what the listener-viewer most deeply knew as "God," and to call that forth in such a way as to make manifest its death, so that the viewer-hearer could experience that death if only momentarily, and could know that experience as life itself. Even in the innumerable university lectures that I gave, and in the many debates in which I engaged, I preached the death of God, believing then and now that this ultimately redemptive event is the very essence of the Christian gospel. If nothing else, I succeeded in giving offense, and this traveling evangelist did experience joy, but only insofar as joy is awakened in others. To what extent that genuinely occurred I cannot know, but I did experience an intense response in others, and a response to what I was proclaiming. While there was certainly nothing original about this, it may well be the first time that it was enacted as preaching through the mass media.

I think that I became one of the most hated men in America. Murder threats were almost a commonplace, savage assaults upon me were widely published, and the churches were seemingly possessed by a fury against me. Yet Archbishop Hallinan of Atlanta publicly and forcefully defended me, and did so in large measure because his confessor was a Trappist monk, Bernard Johnson, who was a dear friend of mine and who became the abbot of the Conyers monastery. The truth is that I was given deep support throughout this period, and while I offended many permanently, and lost every hope of a foundation grant or a major academic appointment, I have never regretted the offense that I gave. A new community opened to me, a community of a wide variety of people, for this country is passionately religious, and at bottom in rebellion at what it has been given as religion. Perhaps the South is most paradoxical at this point. Never did I experience the violent rejection there that I experienced in the North, as epitomized for me when I appeared on *The Merv Griffin Show* in New York, and when I was given exactly two minutes to speak before a live audience in an old Broadway theater. The response was a violent one, forcing the director to close the curtains and order the band to play forcefully, and after this event a crowd greeted me at the stage door, demanding my death. I was only saved from assault by a canny editor who had briefed me for the occasion and then had his taxi backed up to the door.

Let it also be said that the Atlanta newspapers also supported me, just as did many journalists and commentators throughout the country. Innumerable pastors and priests were a source of deep sustenance, and I sensed that I was only saying aloud what many of them knew more deeply. So I became a kind of talisman, of little or no importance in myself, but important to others as their surrogate, or, as many suggested at the time, like the little boy who said aloud what others dared not say, that the emperor has no clothes. Of course, I deeply offended virtually all older theologians, even including Reinhold Niebuhr, but not Paul Tillich. Tillich was my master in meeting and reversing such assaults, but so, too, were Barth and Bultmann, and while I was far from their level as a theologian, I was meeting something like the offense which they provoked, and mine had occurred as a media event, thus if only for this reason it was far more widely known. Of course, this has all now been forgotten—media events vanish almost immediately—but it cannot be denied that for whatever reason theology has subsequently undergone a deep transformation. It is now deeply at the periphery of our culture and society, deeply alien if not simply invisible in our world, and just as at that time many theologians insisted that it was not God but rather theology that had died, this is openly true now. But it is also true theologically that rebirth can only come through death itself, and it remains my hope that theology is even now being reborn through its own death.

It was also during the sixties that America discovered that it was not a Christian nation, to say nothing of being a Protestant one. Not only was this a time when a deep transformation of American anti-Semitism occurred, but the Jewish voice and mind were now first heard in America as integrally and authentically Jewish, and perhaps most forcefully so through my own deep friend and associate, Arthur Cohen. My friendship with Cohen had begun when we were students at the University of Chicago. Just as I had to teach myself theology, he had to teach himself Judaism. While both of us were deeply assisted by others, neither of us could find a home in our institutional religious worlds, nor in our academic worlds. Arthur was even more fully alienated from the academic world than I was, perhaps because his brilliance was purer than mine. He was forced to create his own world, and not only in the world of publishing and writing, but in his own mind and imagination. Cohen is a pure expression of the solitary theologian, and he is certainly one of our most important theologians; indeed, there are those in the Jewish world who think that he simply created Jewish theology, or if not Jewish theology, then an American or postmodern Jewish theology. I believe that his novel, *In the Days of Simon Stern*, is our richest Jewish theological novel, and one of our most profound responses to the Holocaust. Cohen is a truly paradoxical theologian who could know the death of God as an authentic epiphany of Yahweh. Only when the Christian God is dead, and the God of the philosophers as well, can the voice of Yahweh now truly be heard, and it can even be heard in that Holocaust which is the final death of the West, the final ending of our history. Cohen and I engaged in a long correspondence which he once wanted to publish, but I had lost his letters in a basement flood. Yet I shall never lose his deep impact, or his voice and mind as a theologian.

Even the Catholic world now recognizes that the Holocaust, and the subsequent Christian discovery of the Jew, has deeply transformed Christian theology, but so likewise has theology been transformed by its discovery of our deep underworld, the underworld of the poor and the oppressed, the deeply alienated and deeply forgotten, and while this most explicitly occurs in liberation theology, it has much more deeply occurred theologically in an opening to the depths of darkness and abyss. So it is that the theological world has been deeply affected by both Marxism and Freudianism. While I was never a member of the Communist Party, I was deeply engaged with Marxism for many years, and it is a wonder to me that this never was called forth in the days of my assault. Even Anglicanism once had a Communist wing, just as did many of our churches, so liberation theology did not arise out of a void. It was quickly and painlessly absorbed by our established theological world, and this occurred even as that world was ever more deeply becoming conservative and reactionary. Despite all of this, there are genuine Christian Marxists. I was once one myself, and I am not an ex-Marxist in the common sense. I rather think that Marxism is now in a situation not unlike that of Christianity after the end of Christendom, and it may yet undergo its deepest rebirth. Certainly Marxist theologians existed in the sixties well before the birth of liberation theology. Many of them much affected me, and most of all the most creative of Christian Marxist scholars, Norman Gottwald. Despite the fact that Gottwald is surely our most powerful American Old Testament scholar, he was never able to find a genuine university appointment, and as I soon discovered, it is our deepest scholars and thinkers who are most alienated from and alien to our academic world.

Already this was true of Charles Sanders Pierce, by common consent our greatest American philosopher. It is as though America most scorns its deepest sons and daughters; hence the truly American thinker and visionary is by necessity in exile, and while deep exile is known and realized in Europe, it is never so common there as it is in America. Indeed, exiles in the American sense are unknown outside of America. It is here and here alone that actually to exist in one's community is to exist in exile from that community. Certainly I have known exile throughout my theological life, but this is true of all of my real theological friends. We could not imagine being theologians without being in exile, and if this makes possible a genuine theological negation, it is such negation alone which makes possible a true theological affirmation. Obviously this is Hegelian language, and it is Hegel who has most deeply influenced me philosophically, and perhaps theologically as well. I profoundly resisted Hegel for many years, largely under the impact of Kierkegaard, but once I became open to Hegel, I became overwhelmed by his thinking, and this occurred in my first real book, *The New Apocalypse.*

My venture, however, demands a full union of Hegelian and Nietzschean thinking, and while something like this is accomplished by Derrida, and by the Buddhist philosopher Nishitani, as well, mine is a fully theological rather than a philosophical project, even if it demands the incorporation of philosophical thinking. I had never encountered a Hegelian in the theological world—this did not occur until I met Mark

Taylor—and the one Hegel scholar with whom I had studied, Karl Loewith, condemned all possible theological appropriations of Hegel, a condemnation that is dominant in the theological world, again with the exception of the deeper Catholic theological world. Yet the simple truth is, as J. N. Findlay points out, that Hegel is the only philosopher who incorporated the very center of the Christian faith into his deepest thinking, only here that incarnation, crucifixion, and resurrection are realized philosophically, and only here that crucifixion itself, which Hegel could know as an absolute self-emptying or self-negation, is the center of thinking itself. Not only was Hegel the first philosopher to know the death of God, but his philosophical realization of that death in the *Phenomenology of Spirit* created a philosophical revolution, our deepest modern philosophical revolution. If only at this crucial point, Hegel and Nietzsche are united. While they deeply differ in their understanding of the death of God, for each the death of God is apocalypse itself, or an absolute transformation, and the only absolute transformation that has ever actually and historically occurred.

What could a theological appropriation of Hegel mean? In one sense, and perhaps the deepest sense, this is a useless project, for it is already accomplished by Hegel himself, that one thinker since Augustine who fully united philosophical and theological thinking, and did so with such depth that here theology itself seemingly disappears, or is wholly absorbed by philosophical thinking, as even the deepest theological categories are now purely philosophical categories, and it is philosophy and not theology which is here all in all. Yet what Hegel did not give us is an explicit systematic theology, and to the extent that this occurs in his lectures on the philosophy of religion his deeper thinking is abated or disguised. While Hegel began as a theologian, he violently rebelled against the theological world, even while insisting that it was that world and not his own thinking which had betrayed faith itself, so that it is Hegel who launches the first profound and in-depth assault upon theology itself, and does so not upon the periphery but upon the very center of theological thinking. Hegel knew that center with a profundity unequaled by any modern theologian, with the possible exception of Barth, and if Barth is the only full theologian who has succeeded in dissolving all philosophical thinking, this can be understood as a deep response to Hegel, but a response to Hegel that can be reversed, and can be reversed by seeking a Hegelian systematic theology.

I am often asked why I do not write a systematic theology, but actually I have been writing a systematic theology throughout my theological career. What is commonly unrecognized is that a truly new theology demands a new theological language, new theological categories, new theological schemas, and new theological forms, hence it will be wholly unlike all established systematic theologies. Already this is true of Hegel's theological thinking, yet we have not yet appropriated it theologically. Yes, Hegel accomplished that, but we have not, and far more importantly, Hegel thought and wrote before that cataclysmic event which is the end of modernity if not of history itself. This is the real gulf which lies between our world and Hegel's world, so that inevitably Hegelian language and thinking are alien to us, or are so if we cannot unite it with a Nietzschean language and thinking. But if this is possible, and possible for theology itself, then here lies a way to a truly new theology. It very much baffles me that I am now seemingly alone in pursuing such a path. Of course, I once shared this with Mark Taylor, but Taylor has been driven by our new world into a very different path, one which I can only partially recognize as a theological path, yet that could simply mean that I am fully alienated from our new world. Despite the fact that Taylor's present work is in genuine continuity with his previous work, he is now apparently refusing all identification as a theologian, and while that might well be necessary for true theological work today, it is alien to me, because I can only know myself as a theologian.

We live in a world philosophically dominated by the judgment that metaphysics has come to an end, but our philosophy continually enacts this ending. It is as though this is a repetition compulsion in the Freudian sense, for it never succeeds in fully negating metaphysics, a metaphysics seemingly always returning so that it must be negated once again, and perhaps this is most true of the metaphysical God. Few recognize that it is only in the twentieth century that major philosophers have not been theological thinkers, only then that God seemingly disappears from our philosophical language, or is deeply hidden therein. Until Levinas, if even then, there has only been one major twentieth-century philosopher who actually thought about God, and this is Whitehead, although this did not occur until Whitehead moved to America in his final years. Until quite recently, the University of Chicago Divinity School has been the center of Whiteheadian theological thinking, giving us what is commonly known as process or dipolar theology. John Cobb and Schubert Ogden have been its most creative exponents, and Cobb has been the theologian with whom I have conducted the longest theological dialogue. Our correspondence is quite substantial, and is now housed in the library of Syracuse University. In one sense, two theologians could not be as different as John and I are, but in another sense we are much alike: both of us are committed to a genuinely new theology, just as we are committed to philosophical theology, but we are even more deeply alike in seeking a genuinely Buddhist ground, and in seeking an ecumenical theology in the fullest sense. While the death of God is primary in my theology, Cobb parallels this in his full acceptance of the death of every metaphysical God except the Whiteheadian God, and this has grave theological consequences, for it shatters all of our traditional theological understanding.

Cobb has always been my most judicious theological critic. He can enter my theological thinking as few others can, and his criticism is always truly responsible, being creative rather than destructive. It has commonly given me new insight into my own work, new insight opening up new possibilities. I fear that I have not given such criticism to his work, for while I have attempted again and again to do so, it continually eludes me, and this may well say something significant about my own theological isolation. Cobb was once the center of a flourishing theological community at Claremont and beyond, and while this may well be in abeyance today, John was a theological teacher as I was never able to be; his students as I have known them are truly loyal to his work, and it is Cobb who has been the real theological center of the Buddhist-Christian dialogue. I once published an article on the Buddhist ground of the Whiteheadian God in the theological journal which John founded, *Process Studies*, but Cobb goes far beyond this in his thinking. Cobb and I are apparently alone as theologians seeking a Buddhist ground for Christianity, and I suspect that finally we do not deeply differ here; if this is true, we cannot ultimately be theologically apart. Can I say this of any other theologian whom I know? Perhaps, but I would not dare say so openly, for in theology opposition is true friendship. Only in opposition can genuine theological dialogue occur, and only thereby can theology truly advance. What is most missing in our contemporary theological world, or in its manifest expressions, is any commitment to the forward movement of theology. It is as though this could occur only in our ethical or social arenas, and then occur only by the disappearance of actual theological thinking, for in our theological world today it is theology itself which is the deepest enemy, and now it is seemingly being replaced by an apparently total pragmatic thinking, or by an endless critique of theological thinking itself.

Robert Scharlemann is the philosophical theologian who once most engaged me, and I regard his *The Being of God: Theology and the Experience of Truth* as a truly seminal theological work. Here not only are philosophical and theological thinking truly united, but the Crucifixion is unraveled in thinking itself, and in pure thinking itself. Scharlemann is the most isolated theologian whom I know, and also the one in the deepest exile, and possibly the deepest solitude, and this despite his real power as a teacher. He has always been deeply alienated from the academic departments in which he has been forced to reside, as is evident in his recently forced retirement from the University of Virginia. No one could be personally or publicly less offensive than Bob. it is as though he is simply incapable of giving offense, and yet he has clearly been profoundly offensive, and most offensive to those who are most confident or secure theologically. Here is someone who not only deeply knows theology, and knows it in faith, but this is a knowledge deeply lacerating to virtually all theologies, for this is a critique truly within, and within faith itself. Scharlemann's formula, "the being of God when God is not being God," is not simply an assault upon the metaphysical God, but upon every Godhead manifest apart from the Crucifixion, which is to say upon every Godhead which theology commonly knows, and while Bob has chosen Heidegger as his philosophical mentor, he repudiates Heidegger's own theology insofar as it is ascertainable, seeking a Heideggerian thinking beyond Heidegger himself. Perhaps this should be the path of every philosophical theology, just as it is in Augustine's relation to Plato, in Aquinas's relation to Aristotle, and hopefully in Altizer's relation to Hegel and Nietzsche.

Why is the academic world so inhospitable to theology today? Of course, this is true of the church, too, which apparently leaves theology without a home, but perhaps theology has always been most deeply homeless, an abandoned orphan in the world, and most abandoned where it is seemingly most needed. We long said this of the communist world, but is it really different in the capitalist world, in our world, in America, and in that America which is supposedly the most religious country in the industrial world? It was Barth himself who first established theology as the deepest enemy of religion, a primal position which has disappeared in that Barthianism that now dominates Protestant theology, so now we have a toothless theology, a theology wholly incapable of giving offense, and perhaps for that very reason it is now irrelevant and lifeless. Yet the Catholic hierarchy can know theology as a true enemy, just as does our secular academic world, and perhaps there is hope in that, and as I look back upon the hope that we theologians once had, I try to recapture its original ground, for I refuse to believe that it was simply illusory, or only a product of our pride, and seek instead to recover what was once a source of such hope, which certainly seemed to be overwhelmingly real at that time.

It was nontheologians who originally gave me the deepest theological hope, nontheologians who knew far more deeply than I did that ultimate crisis which had become our destiny, a crisis shattering modernity itself, and therefore dissolving modernity's comprehensive negation of theology itself. This does not mean that it is possible to return to a premodern theology; it rather means that there is an overwhelming demand for a new theology, a new theology already latent in the hidden or disguised theological expressions of modernity itself, theological expressions alien to all established theology, but nevertheless overwhelmingly theological in their very depth. I found that it was literary scholars who were most deeply unveiling this, discovering in our most profound literature a religious or ultimate vision that is simply inexplicable through our given theological categories. Here was a deep treasure, indeed, but we could not understand it theologically, or, insofar as this occurred, it occurred as an ultimate challenge to all established theological understanding. Then I discovered that many of our great writers were themselves deeply theological, and not only in their interior lives, but in the very depths of their greatest creations. This is manifest for all to see in our great Christian epics, but also in our seemingly most anti-religious visionaries, such as Proust, Beckett, and Stevens. Eric Heller, Northrop Frye, Georges

Poulet, and J. Hillis Miller all taught me this, but I learned it far more intimately through Gregor Sebba and Walter Strauss, and when I finally became a professor of English at the State University of New York at Stony Brook, I found that I had been appointed simply because I was a theologian, for it is literature itself which demands a theological explication.

It was at Stony Brook that I truly began an exploration of the Christian epic tradition, for my book on Blake had treated Blake as an isolated visionary. I had no full realization then of the integral relationship between Blake and Milton, or of what I only gradually discovered as the deep relationship between Blake and Joyce. Once these became established, it becomes possible to see the Christian epic as one epic, and as one integral and organic epic, and even if there is a vast distance between Dante and Joyce, it is possible to apprehend an organic evolution occurring between them, an evolution that is, of course, a deeply imaginative voyage, but it is no less so a theological voyage. If I made any literary contribution at all in my exploration, it was in calling forth a theological interpretation of *Finnegans Wake*. Now it is not insignificant theologically that all of our great Christian epics poets are deeply heretical; indeed, it is only here that we can discover the depths of heresy, or of a uniquely modern heresy. Even Nietzsche pales in the wake of *Finnegan's Wake,* and what a joy it was to discover Milton's *De Doctrina Christiana*, a book totally ignored in the theological world, and a book not only inseparable from *Paradise Lost*, but one which is a truly biblical theology, and yet only truly biblical by being profoundly heretical. It is our poets who are our deepest heretics—Plato did not irresponsibly ban them from the state—and it is our literary scholars who are our deepest academic heretics, as manifest in the American Deconstructionist movement, which here so deeply differs from its French ground.

I also interpret the Christian epic tradition as an apocalyptic tradition, and what could be a greater challenge to the theological movement of Demythologizing, for that apocalyptic ground which is here demythologized is now apprehended as being profoundly reborn in our epic voyage, an epic voyage comprehending simultaneously the interior and the cosmic voyages of modernity, and if it can be demonstrated that this is truly an apocalyptic voyage, then apocalypticism is universal in our world as it never was in the ancient world, and just as apocalypticism is more manifest today than ever previously in our history, the apocalypticism of the New Testament itself is a decisive way into our world, even if this is unknown to every New Testament scholar. Now these are exciting theological possibilities, and my literary colleagues react to them seriously as my theological colleagues do not, largely I fear because theologians simply cannot believe that theology might accomplish so much. In many ways theologians are their own worst enemies, for we find it impossible to believe that we have been given such opportunities, impossible to believe in the grace of theology itself. But how is it possible to deny the very glory of the epic visions of Dante, Milton, Blake, and Joyce? And if this is truly an apocalyptic glory, and an apocalyptic joy, then theology has been given a key to this glory and joy, and what could be a greater theological hope?

By this time I was publicly invisible as a theologian, and also invisible to the great bulk of the theological world, but I was now engaged in my most important work, and I had a confidence that I had never known before; all too gradually a comprehensive vision came to possess me, and I simply could not conceive of the possibility of doing anything more decisive, and of anything more decisive for theology itself. Only seldom did I now speak publicly, and my preaching days were over, or over except for my teaching and writing, for mine continues to be a homiletic theology at bottom, and I will always be a Southern preacher. My friends in our literary and philosophical worlds find nothing odd about this, even if theologians do, and again and again I have discovered that the secular world wants us to be theologians; if nothing else we are as such strange creatures in the academic world, and even if that world can become hostile when we are too theological, and can recognize an enemy when theology is truly theological, it is just when we are most openly enemies that we discover our deepest friends, for conformist as the academic world surely is, it also thrives on and through heretics, and true theology is inevitably deeply heretical. But the same could be said of genuine science, and at Stony Brook it was the ruling scientists who were my firmest academic political allies. Just as they looked upon philosophy, literary hermeneutics, and theology as being equally unscientific, it was they alone who were there open to the deepest challenge, and they appeared to relish such challenge when it came from me.

I was the only theologian at Stony Brook. Indeed, I thought of myself then as the only real theologian in the world of the greater New York area, for by this time both the Union Theological Seminary and the Yale Divinity School had collapsed or reversed themselves; Princeton and Yale were then, as they are now, centers of a dead or frozen theological orthodoxy. This was the challenge, which Ray Hart assumed as the opportunity of establishing a truly new theological world. I had served as the vice-chairman of the executive committee of the faculty senate at Stony Brook, and my weak academic politicking did succeed in establishing a new and major religious studies chair at Stony Brook; I chose Ray for this position, not because I then knew him intimately, but rather because I knew he was a real theologian, and I deeply admired him for his transformation of *The Journal of the American Academy of Religion*, and his transformation of the American Academy of Religion itself. Ray was ambitious for theology as few if any have been, and I knew that he could act forcefully in leading the theological and religious studies world ahead. I did not expect him to refuse the professorship, but instead he chose to use its funds to establish a full and comprehensive study of the opportunities before us, leading to a plan to establish a center of graduate religious studies at Stony Brook, both serving the New York City area, and establishing networks throughout the State University of New York.

I think that this was the most ambitious plan for religious studies ever formulated in America or perhaps the world. Soon we were negotiating with both the Jewish Theological Seminary and the Woodstock Theological Seminary of the Society of Jesus to join us, and there was the bonus of the move to Stony Brook of the Institute for the Advanced Study of World Religions, a Buddhist scholarly and meditative institute which already had a serious publishing program, and it was even more ambitious than we could imagine. And we had the deep support of Elizabeth Luce Moore, the chairman of the board of trustees of the State University of New York, and a real power in her own right. Soon we were joined by Patrick Heelan, an Irish Jesuit philosopher of science, who as chairman had transformed our philosophy department and was now a major administrator at Stony Brook. Everything seemed to be moving beautifully, and while real problems did arise, such as the failure of both of the seminaries to join us, we probably would have succeeded, but just at that time the war in

Vietnam ended, and in the consequent recession, which particularly affected New York, the state education budget was radically cut and the opportunity for all new programs simply vanished. It was Ray who was the decisive leader in all of this, and while we had exciting planning committee meetings with an international team of distinguished religious scholars, and meetings and serious programs throughout both the city and the state of New York, all of it finally came to nothing, and the chair which Ray again refused was wisely offered to Robert Neville.

Nevertheless, this was a period of excitement for me. We did have a truly major plan seriously in place, and it entailed not simply an interdisciplinary program, but an integration of Eastern and Western traditions, a full incorporation of Judaica with the intention of later incorporating Islam, an understanding of theology as a universal discipline with a fully philosophical ground, and the further intention of drawing major writers and artists from New York into the program as it evolved. Throughout this period there were innumerable conversations and conferences with a wide variety of thinkers and scholars. We always met with full support, and it was simply impossible to question that there was a huge potential here, and one meeting an overwhelming need. In this context, the traditional seminary or school of religion simply seemed to be anachronistic, and we were amazed that we met no real opposition to this venture; it is as though such a project was simply an inevitable consequence of the advent of that new world which was now fully at hand. Certainly such forces were at play. The academic world was in fact becoming more interdisciplinary and more ecumenical, Christianity and biblical studies were ceasing to be the center of religious studies in the country as a whole, and theology in the university world was ever more fully distancing itself from religious institutions and traditions, just as the very distinction between the sacred and the profane or the religious and the secular was not only becoming anachronistic but was even reversing itself. Who could doubt that we were truly entering a new world? And how could we not be caught up in a joyous and even ecstatic hope?

CHAPTER 3

Epic Theology

When such a hope collapses, it does not leave in its wake a simple void or surd, it rather can call forth a new determination, a new resolution to accomplish such an intention in the microscopic world of one's own work, and even if that should have no reverberations beyond itself, and no apparent contact with a larger world, it does make possible a voyage which is intended to be a total voyage, and a voyage into the depths of that to which one has been called. A false start occurred in my *The Descent into Hell*, a book written much too rapidly, and much too easily, and although I now believe that the direction here is the right one, and its theological movement a responsible one, real agony and real joy are missing here, and hence real substance as well. But the book does call forth that *coincidentia oppositorum* between Buddhism and Christianity which became essential to my work. Even then I sensed that something had gone deeply wrong. Its language is not a real language, and that very hollowness belies its fundamental movement, so that I knew that I must find a new language, and this could be possible only by way of a new voyage. Years ago I had attempted and failed a monastic vocation; again and again I had attempted Buddhist meditation, and in fact had come under the influence of true contemporary masters of Buddhism, but I had come to believe that such ways were not for me. So likewise I had come to believe that there is a poetic meditation which is fully parallel to sacred meditation, that the deep poet inevitably not only calls for but enacts such meditation, therein making possible for others their own individual voyage into the depths, and that the true teacher of poetry is one who makes possible for his or her students such a voyage. Moreover, I was persuaded that theological writing can and must follow a parallel path. Augustine's *Confessions* has always been my favorite theological book, and it is a book fully uniting theological and meditative thinking, and perhaps for that very reason it has had a deeper impact than any other theological book.

I know that *The Self-Embodiment of God* is my best book, but I equally know that it is not truly my own. It certainly came as a gift, one wholly unexpected and gratuitous, and even if it also came out of a long and deep struggle, and only after the closing of many false paths, it is a book which in a genuine sense wrote itself, so that it is not simply the product of this author; and it is unquestionably beyond every intention which I brought to its writing. I well remember the site of this writing, the dining room of my Victorian house in Port Jefferson on Long Island, where I wrote while standing because of problems with my lower back. I shall also never forget that Ray Hart and Bob Funk were visiting me while I was completing its first chapter, and when they returned from a visit to Montauk Point, I proclaimed in shock that this chapter on genesis had finally proven the existence of God: Bob immediately said, "Rush upstairs and take two baths!"

The truth is that genuine theological writing does demand a lustration or purification. Perhaps all genuine writing does. It is not insignificant that none of our primal original prophets were writers, for real writing is a violation, and even is so in its most ecstatic modes. This is most clearly true of theological writing, where even the writing of the word "God" is a violation; Judaism is not alone in condemning this, and the theologian who can write of God without a deep sense of violation is simply not a real theologian. I certainly had an overwhelming sense of violation in writing *The Self-Embodiment of God*, and far more so than in any of my previous writing, which might appear odd, since I had so often written of the death of God, but the great difference is that this book is far more truly writing than is any of my previous writing, and it is also, and perhaps just thereby, far more deeply theological, and in being theological in a full sense it is precisely thereby violation.

A word is in order about the intentions that were originally brought to this book, which were extraordinarily ambitious. First, there was the intention of writing a full biblical theology, which had seemingly become impossible in the twentieth century, and even more impossible in the late twentieth century. A genuine biblical theology cannot avoid biblical scholarship, or simply suspend it, as Barth does in his *Church Dogmatics*, and it is precisely biblical scholarship which has most made biblical theology impossible. True, biblical theology deeply occurs in Bultmann's *Theology of the New Testament*, but here it can occur only by way of a radical demythologizing deeply transforming eschatological into existential categories, thus finally negating the historical and linguistic world of the New Testament. It is not wholly irresponsible to identify Demythologizing as a contemporary form of Gnosticism, for it does transform the historical into the "spiritual" or the "existential" (or *Historie* into *Geschichte*), just as it transforms apocalypticism into a contemporary authenticity. Moreover, biblical scholarship in its deepest expressions has been ultimately radical, as most clearly manifest in Bultmannianism, and in the era in which I was writing *The Self-Embodiment of God*. Biblical scholarship simply was radical scholarship, or certainly so in those circles that most affected me, and theologically this means that it was far distant from everything that we can understand theologically. While those biblical scholars who were closest to me were all theological thinkers, none of them could think in any given theological language, and all repudiated anything which could possibly be a systematic theology, or certainly any systematic theology claiming to be a biblical theology.

Second, there was the intention in this book to write a theology that would be Eastern and Western at once, or Buddhist and Christian at once, and while inevitably this theology would be far more Christian than Buddhist, it was essential here to call forth a biblical theology that would be absolutely groundless or empty apart from a deep and primordial Buddhist or Eastern ground. This occurs immediately in the book in its exploration of silence, and its first chapter on genesis or absolute beginning calls forth genesis as an original self-emptying or self-negation of an absolute silence which is an absolute nothingness or an absolute emptiness, or what the Buddhist knows as Sunyata; just as its last chapter on apocalypse calls forth apocalypse as the dawning of the full actuality of an absolute silence, an absolute silence which is Sunyata and Kingdom of God at once. I was deeply gratified when a leading Buddhologist, Lewis Lancaster, at a Stony Brook colloquium unexpectedly presented an exegesis of *The Self-Embodiment of God* as though it were a Buddhist Sutra, and I like to think that this was not wholly ironic. Nishitani and Abe gave me every encouragement to move in this direction, they are primal representatives of that Kyoto School which had incorporated Western philosophical and theological categories into its new Buddhist philosophy, and I intended *The Self-Embodiment of God* to be a parallel expression of a Western ecumenical theology.

Finally, there was the intention of writing a meditational theology that would incorporate a Hegelian movement of pure negativity into a purely meditative form. The primal categories here are speech and silence, and the movement from silence to speech to a final silence is intended to embody the biblical movement from genesis to apocalypse, but to do so in such a way that it is not only renewed but reenacted by the reader. While this is a transformation of the historical into the interior, it is intended to embody the full actuality of the historical into this very movement, and to draw forth its biblical centers, such as the prophetic revolution, in their full historical actuality, even if here they are realized only internally or meditationally. A crucial question would be, does this movement actually embody such centers, or, even more concretely, could the historian recognize the listening which is here enacted as a recapitulation of a uniquely prophetic listening and response? I would like to think that this book at bottom is more historical than is Bultmann's *Theology of the New Testament*, or is so in its theological language, and this despite the fact that Bultmann is a great historian whereas this author is no real historian at all. But just as fundamental here is the intention of calling forth the biblical movement as one movement, so that its New Testament and Old Testament poles are fully integrated, and not only fully integrated, but fully pass into each other, and do so by way of a Hegelian pure negativity that simultaneously both affirms and negates every division and opposition of both consciousness and history at once. Perhaps Hegel's supreme achievement was his full integration of consciousness and history, so that even the *Science of Logic* is finally a deeply historical work, and, if so, this does make possible a theology fully integrating history and consciousness, an integration in which history itself is at bottom both negated and affirmed.

Gnosticism is a pure and total negation of history, and a concrete test of the possible Gnostic ground of any work is whether or not it effects such a negation. There are at least two points within this book wherein such a test may be employed. The first is its enactments of Jesus and the prophets. The test would be as to whether or not their historical grounds are here preserved. While both the prophets and Jesus are presented as being genderless (which no feminist has observed), they are genderless because they are faceless, but they are not voiceless (as opposed to Gnosticism!). On the contrary, here their voice is all in all, and this is a voice embodying an absolute eschatological judgment which is an absolute eschatological transfiguration, and, as opposed to Gnosticism again, this is a judgment and transfiguration which is dialectical rather than dualistic, wherein the negated is not simply obliterated or dissolved but rather itself passes into its own contrary or opposite. But perhaps the most crucial test of Gnosticism derives from the question of the presence or absence of the biblical God. Is God the Creator present or absent, and is this presence or absence decisive for the work in question? I would affirm that God the Creator is present here, and if a self-negation or self-emptying of the Creator does occur, it occurs not by way of a dissolution, but rather by way of God's own act, an act which is absolute sacrifice itself, but that sacrifice is a fulfillment of the Creator, in which the Godhead itself is even more fully and more finally itself.

Perhaps this does not in fact occur in the book, or is not enacted in the book, and if so the book is finally a failure. But it can be read in such a way that it occurs, even if here the reader must transcend the author; thus the book does demand a meditational reading, a reading in which the reader actually enacts what occurs, although this may well force the reader to respond to this text as an anti-text, a text annulling or reversing the enactment for which it calls. While the book has had few readers, it has engendered a deep response in certain quarters, which I fear were responses to its intentions rather than to its text alone, and one of these drew forth an identity for which I longed but could never dare openly affirm: and that is that the book belongs within the sacred circle of the Torah. This identification occurs in a preface by Jacob Neusner to a republication of the book by the University Press of America, in a series that he edits, Brown Classics of Judaica. Neusner, himself a truly major historian, can go on to say that the book is a profound rereading of the Torah's account of the meaning and end of history. Yes, I hope that this book is a Torah theology, and if we have finally learned that Christian theology must be a Torah theology, it can only be so in a truly new world.

It would appear that this book is at a vast distance from that Christian epic tradition which is so fundamental for my work, but at least one literary critic did respond to *The Self-Embodiment of God* as a poem, and I have discovered that sections can have far more of an impact when they are heard orally, so I sense that the voice of the preacher is not silent here. And it was only after the writing or receiving of this book that I could fully execute my quest for the Christian epic; indeed, I believe that only this book made possible *History as Apocalypse*, my book on the Christian epic, a book that attempts a reenactment of our Christian epics, although in an abbreviated and non-poetic mode. One challenge here is to understand our epic poetry as revelation itself, and while I think that it is clear that this was the actual intention of all of our great epic writers, epics can only be heard or read as revelation when they are responded to as repetitions of the Bible itself. It is remarkable how biblical our Christian epics are; they are far more biblical than any other books in our tradition, and I believe more truly biblical than any of our theological writing. A re-saying of the words of the Bible should not be thought of as a literal repetition of these words; it is far more so a repetition in the Kierkegaardian sense, a forward rather than a backward movement, and a forward movement into the truly new. Certainly that occurs in our great Christian epics, each of which is explosively new, thus apocalyptically new; apocalypse is the deepest center of our Christian epics, and here occurs a rebirth and renewal of the biblical apocalypse which has never occurred in our theology.

It is odd that so little theological interpretation has been given to our epic texts, and when it does occur it commonly does so through a traditional theological interpretation, thus clearly violating the texts themselves; for not only are these deeply heretical texts, but each is a reversal of the theological orthodoxy of their historical worlds, and above all a reversal of everything that their worlds could theologically know as God. While this is most comprehensive in Joyce, it is clearest in Blake, perhaps most powerful in Milton, and most ecstatically joyous in Dante. Yet the ecstatic joy of the conclusion of the *Purgatorio* and the *Paradiso* is inseparable from the deepest darkness of the *Inferno*, just as the absolutely alien sovereignty of the Creator is inseparable from the absolute sacrifice of the Son in *Paradise Lost*, a dialectical polarity and union repeated but now universalized in *Milton* and *Jerusalem*, just as it is this very union and polarity which is absolutely reversed and comprehensively repeated in *Ulysses* and *Finnegans Wake*. Few interpreters realize the depth of the presence of God in the *Wake* and *Ulysses*, for even if this is an absolutely sacrilegious and blasphemous presence, it is a total presence nonetheless, as a primordial fall of God or Satan is continually reenacted in an ecstatic celebration, finally culminating in the apocalypse of Molly or Anna Livia Plurabelle, who is an epic repetition of Blake's Jerusalem and Dante's Beatrice.

History as Apocalypse attempts to call forth the ultimate union of our Christian epics, a union which is the unity of the Bible itself, but now a union realized in the actuality of our history and consciousness, and if it is possible to understand both a beginning and ending of consciousness, this is enacted in our epic tradition from Homer through Joyce. Just as an individually actual voice first occurs or is first manifest in *The Iliad*, a universal reversal and ending of all voice occurs in *Finnegans Wake*. Here, too, is genesis and apocalypse, and a genesis and apocalypse of our uniquely Western history, whose very ending is the advent of a universal humanity and a universal world. In *History as Apocalypse*, each of our great epics is understood as a consequence and an embodiment of a new revolutionary era, each is the expression of a new revolutionary transformation of consciousness and society, but these very transformations are finally in organic continuity with each other, comprising one comprehensive and evolutionary movement. This is why our great epics are finally one epic, and one universal epic, for not only is the epic hero finally Here Comes Everybody, but Here Comes Everybody is finally that Buddha or Christ which is totality itself, and a fully actual or fully realized totality.

There is one new theological movement in *History as Apocalypse* which is uniquely its own, and that is a movement into Satan, and while this certainly occurs in *The New Apocalypse*, it occurs there only through a Blakean Satan who is the absolutely alien Creator. Now there is an attempt to explore that Satan who evolves in the Christian epic, and to understand the evolution of Satan in our imagination and history as the dialectical contrary of the evolution of Christ. Here, *Paradise Lost* made possible the deepest breakthrough for me, that

Paradise Lost in which Satan and the Son of God are dialectical polarities, each essential to the other, and each only actually realized by their opposition to the other. This is true both in Satan's expulsion from Heaven, and the Son's choice of Crucifixion, that crucifixion which is the sole source of an apocalyptic redemption, and an apocalyptic redemption that is inseparable from the eternity of Hell. At last I had also moved into that predestination which later was to become so central in my thinking, for not only is predestination here a predestination both to Heaven and to Hell, or a double predestination, but each is essential to the other. Indeed, each is unreal apart from the other, so that Satan is just as essential to redemption as is Christ, and this is a consequence of an original enactment by Godhead itself. Therefore that Godhead could only be a truly dialectical Godhead, a dialectical Godhead in which an absolute Yes-saying and an absolute No-saying are not only inseparable, but finally indistinguishable from each other.

While such a Godhead is not fully called forth, or unmistakably called forth, until the culmination of our epic tradition in *Finnegans Wake*, the deep ground of this movement is already fully manifest in the essential relationship between the *Paradiso* and the *Inferno*, and even if Dante's Satan is silent and immobile except for his eternal consumption of a trinity of sinners, he is the absolute ruler of Hell, and the final source of evil itself; and just as Dante was the first poet fully or truly to enact pure evil, this enactment in the *Commedia* is absolutely essential to its truly new vision of Heaven, a Heaven truly different from every possible primordial Heaven. For it is a Heaven that is not only an absolute actuality, but a Heaven that is the consequence of a divine and cosmic movement, and for the first time in the Christian tradition Godhead itself can be envisioned as being inseparable from the cosmos or the world itself. The very actuality of this Heaven can be known by way of its essential relation to Hell, and just as the *Purgatorio* and the *Paradiso* are impossible and unreal apart from the *Inferno*, Dante's Heaven is illusory and unreal apart from the horizon of Hell, and all too significantly it is only in the *Inferno* that Dante can call forth the full individuality of the human voice and face. Only in the *Inferno* is Dante a fully realistic poet, and it is the very depth of this realism that is echoed or reflected in the cosmic ground, and the uniquely cosmic ground, of Dante's Heaven.

We have always known that Dante is a revolutionary poet and visionary, but we have not understood that this is inseparable from a revolutionary theological ground, one truly and deeply heretical. Nor is this simply because of Dante's vision of an empire that is the equal of the church, but because of his epic vision itself, a vision uniquely integrating the ecclesiastical, the political, the psychological, and the cosmic realms, but so integrating them that they are inseparable from the divine realm itself. This is an absolutely new realism, indeed, and a truly new understanding of the Godhead itself. It can justly be said that Dante far more deeply integrates nature and grace than does Aquinas, and he certainly does so far more comprehensively, and if it has truly been said that the *Commedia* is the *summa* of the Christian Middle Ages, dare we say that it is the true *summa theologica* of that world? Aquinas himself gives little actual attention to the question of evil as opposed to the question of sin, largely repeating Augustine, but not only is evil overwhelming in the *Inferno*; this is a truly new vision and understanding of evil, and as opposed to every scholastic understanding of evil as the privation of the good, here evil is intrinsically and essentially real. For even if Hell is the realm of the shades, it could not possibly be understood here as a pure nothingness. Its very realism is far too overwhelming for that, and only here does Dante write with an actuality that can be fully and actually heard, or heard by us. Therefore this is an actuality absolutely essential to that apocalyptic redemption which is now first fully envisioned.

Nothing more clearly distinguishes a uniquely modern vision than does its deep ground in evil, or in a pure negativity, a pure negativity wholly unknown in the ancient world, or in a pre-Christian world, and if Christianity is unique in its vision of Satan, damnation, and Hell, so, too, is a Christian naming of Satan unique, one inaugurated by Jesus himself, and one which is a dominant motif throughout the New Testament, even as it is absent from every pre-Christian scripture. Nietzsche was fully responsible in knowing that it is Christianity alone which embodies an absolute No-saying, and in the Christian epic that absolute No-saying is essentially inseparable from an absolute Yes-saying, and only in Christianity are an absolute No-saying and an absolute Yes-saying fully conjoined, an ultimate union which is deeply and continually called forth in the Christian epic, and at no other point is Joyce's epic vision so clearly and so manifestly Christian. Yet this is just the point at which the deep realism of Christianity is manifest, one that has never been understood theologically, but which is deeply embodied in the Christian epic vision and the Christian epic voyage, for if this is a voyage into the deepest chaos and darkness, such a voyage is here and here alone inseparable from a voyage into an ecstatic life and joy. Hence the absolute necessity of Satan in Christianity, and just as the Christian epic voyage ever more fully and more finally calls forth epiphanies of Satan, these epiphanies are here essential to epiphanies of Christ; and if in Blake and Joyce Satan is envisioned as being all in all, that totality of Satan is inseparable from the totality of Christ, or inseparable from that Christ who is apocalyptic totality itself.

If a *coincidentia oppositorum* between Christ and Satan is a deep center of the Christian epic, it only gradually evolves or become manifest, not being fully called forth until full modernity, and only full modernity has envisioned the totality of Hell, or an absolute abyss or total darkness, a vision of the ultimate and final depths of an absolutely alien abyss that can be discovered in every primal expression of the late modern imagination. I first met Langdon Gilkey after having heard him give a stunning lecture in which he demonstrated the absence of damnation and Hell in every modern theology. I was deeply shaken by this, which baffled Langdon, for I simply could not imagine how it is possible to be a genuine theologian without a deep sense of damnation, and if only at this point there is an ultimate chasm between modern and premodern theology. Strange as it may appear, many theologians consider me to be deeply conservative theologically, and I certainly am so at this point, but again and again I wonder how it is possible to be open to the modern imagination and to have no sense of damnation and Hell. Surely our imaginative world, or our deeper imaginative world, is far more possessed by damnation than is any previous imaginative world, and yet modern theology proceeds in indifference to this, and this despite the horrors of our century. It is true that our deeper modern theology has been truly affected by Kierkegaard's unveiling of *Angst* or dread as an encounter with the Nothing, and that there is a crucial section of Barth's *Church Dogmatics* which calls forth the Nihil or the Nothing in this spirit. So, too, Tillich wrestled with the Nothing throughout a substantial portion of his work. Nevertheless our theologians have remained silent about Satan and Hell, and Barth, the one major modern theologian who has truly thought about damnation, has denied its possibility as a consequence of the victory of Christ.

Has our theology nothing to say about our darkness and abyss? Is this a fundamental reason why our theological language about redemption is so hollow and unreal? How is it possible to understand redemption if we cannot understand damnation? In classical theology redemption is always redemption from damnation, a damnation which is universal as a consequence of the fall, and every classical theologian is a theologian of damnation; but in modern theology damnation has disappeared, and with that disappearance is it possible to know redemption at all? And how can Christ truly be known apart from Satan? There is surely no such understanding of Christ in the New Testament, or in the Christian world until the full advent of modernity, yet the modern imagination has known Satan far more deeply and comprehensively than any previous imagination, and nowhere more so than in the modern Christian epic. Satan can be understood as the dominant figure in *Finnegans Wake*. A primordial fall of Satan occurs on its first page, a fall which is continually repeated throughout this epic, and the *Wake* culminates in a glorious apocalypse; and if its closing lines pass immediately into its opening lines, this is an absolute apocalypse inseparable and indistinguishable from an absolute fall, so that a Joycean apocalypse, even as a Dantean apocalypse, is intrinsically real, but real only within the horizon of fall and darkness, or only within the horizon of what we can only name as Satan. The centrality of Satan in our modern epics does distinguish them from the *Commedia*. It is even possible to understand Satan as the true epic hero of all of our modern epics, and therein the modern epic hero is a tragic hero, as we see so forcefully in our great American epic, *Moby-Dick*; but can a uniquely modern Satan be understood as an atoning Satan, as a sacrificial victim whose pure evil draws all evil into itself, so that the sacrifice of this Satan is the deepest possible assuagement, the deepest possible reconciliation, the deepest possible atonement? That could be nothing less than an apocalyptic atonement, one already envisioned in the Book of Revelation, and the Book of Revelation is truly primary in all of our great Christian epics, even as it is absent in virtually all of our modern theology.

A deep rediscovery of Satan already occurs in Boehme's vision, one which played a decisive role in the advent of German Idealism, and even if Lucifer or Satan is a minor figure in Hegel's writing, it is Hegel above all other modern thinkers who knows a pure and absolute negativity. Indeed, at no other point is Hegel so unique as a philosophical thinker, and it is a Hegelian negativity, even if a reverse Hegelian negativity, which is the deepest foundation of the revolutionary thinking of Kierkegaard and Marx, just as it is reborn once again in the revolutionary thinking of Nietzsche. And it is Nietzsche above all other thinkers who most deeply understood damnation, understanding it as that new and absolute nothingness which is a consequence of the death of God, an absolute nothingness which is the very arena of a uniquely modern eternal recurrence, and if this new Zarathustra's eternal recurrence is a total and final Yes-saying, that is an absolute Yes-saying inseparable from an absolute No-saying, or inseparable from an opening to the deepest depths of *ressentiment* or damnation, and only an absolute affirmation of those depths makes possible a final or apocalyptic Yes. Yet this is precisely that apocalyptic Yes which we can discover in the epic enactments of Blake and Joyce, enactments wholly unreal apart from the advent of a truly new Satan, or a truly new darkness and abyss; and just as Jesus named Satan and Hell as did no previous prophet, Blake and Joyce have named Satan as have no other modern prophets, a naming which is truly a rebirth of a Miltonic naming of Satan, but now Satan can be known as a totality never previously manifest, although its full potentiality resides in Dante's epic enactment of Hell.

Never must we lose sight of the epic voyage of the *Commedia*, a voyage whose epic hero is Dante or a universal humanity, and a voyage that can only begin as a voyage into Hell, a voyage in which we actually taste, and see, and hear damnation, and now hear it with an immediacy that we have never heard before. The *Commedia* could only have been written in the vernacular, a deep epic innovation, for this is a language that is intended to be open to everyone, and if everyone does not know Purgatory or Heaven, everyone does know Hell, for everyone is damned to Hell, and thus everyone who is open to depth itself is open to Hell. Only a voyage to Hell makes possible a voyage to Purgatory and Heaven; only a passage through the deepest darkness makes possible a voyage to the deepest light; and just as the elect in Purgatory and Heaven are elect because they are redeemed from Hell, the ecstatic glory of Heaven is an apocalyptic reversal of the horror and darkness of Hell, and just as the apocalyptic vision of Heaven in the Book of Revelation is inseparable from its apocalyptic vision of Hell, Dante's vision of Heaven is inseparable from his vision of Hell, so that to read the *Paradiso* alone is not to read the *Commedia* at all. One of the deep ironies for us in the *Commedia* is Purgatory itself, a purgatory that was not fully or truly born until the Christian Middle Ages, and which has seemingly vanished today; yet Dante is perhaps most original in the *Purgatorio*, or most original theologically. Only here is he open to the possibility of redemption for the pagan world, and only here does he portray purification or atonement, and horrible as that purification may be, it is a joyous purification, and one accepted as such by those who suffer it. Indeed, the joy here is a far more human joy than the joy that Dante calls forth in the *Paradiso*, a joy that we can know and feel, and know it as we cannot know the apocalyptic joy of the *Paradiso*.

Yet if we have lost Purgatory, we have surely lost Dante's Heaven. But have we lost it? Can we discover it in our modern Christian epics, and, above all, can we discover it in the deeply Catholic epics of Joyce? If Purgatory is most deeply an actual process of purification or atonement, an atoning process whose inevitable destiny is Heaven itself, yet a Heaven hidden throughout this process, is this not a process that we can recognize as occurring in *Ulysses* and *Finnegans Wake*? Here, it occurs in the full actuality of our days and nights, and this is a truly prosaic or worldly actuality, for Joyce created a truly new vernacular language to express this actuality, the first epic language to record the absolutely common, that absolutely common or absolutely universal humanity which is Here Comes Everybody. Perhaps a decisive reason why it is so extraordinarily difficult to enter Joyce's epics theologically is that we have lost all understanding of Purgatory. One could search in vain for a truly modern Catholic understanding of Purgatory, and only one out of almost eight hundred pages is given to Purgatory in the only modern *Catechism of the Catholic Church* (1994). If the Catholic believes that purgatory occurs only after death, this is a belief that is certainly alien to Joyce, unless the *Wake* is a celebration of eternal death, and of an eternal death that is an eternal life and joy. Certainly the days and nights of *Ulysses* and of

Finnegans Wake are truly and ultimately purgatorial; here the *Purgatorio* is truly reborn, and reborn as it is nowhere else in our imaginative vision. Yet, this, too, is an apocalyptic rebirth, hence this is an apocalyptic purgatory, and it is overwhelmingly realistic to us as the *Purgatorio* can never be, or can never be apart from its rebirth here.

How ironic that our imaginative vision should be so richly theological whereas our theological thinking is so constricted and confined. Is there an essential relationship between these distant poles? Is it the very poverty of our theological thinking which makes possible the treasures of our theological imagination, the very death of theology which makes possible the ecstatic life of the imagination? Such would appear to be true in the fullness of the modern world, yet both Dante and Milton were genuine theological thinkers, and it is possible to correlate Blake's vision with Hegel's dialectical thinking and Joyce's vision with Nietzsche's revolutionary thinking, as I have attempted to do. So it is possible that we could discover a theology incorporating the modern imagination, and there is surely no greater theological task at hand. Nor could this possibly be accomplished by any kind of apologetics. Barth should be celebrated for so forcefully repudiating all theological apologetics. No, it is dogmatic or systematic or fundamental theology which must become open to the imagination, and open to that revolutionary theological vision already embodied in our great imaginative creations.

CHAPTER 4

Initiation

From the Second World War until quite recently American theology has been at least implicitly radical; at no other point does it differ more clearly from European theology. During this period there have been virtually no American theologians of repute or power who have been church theologians, or not with the exception of ethics (commonly the domain of the conservative mind), and one consequence of this has been that during this period American churches have become theologically groundless, a void that has been filled by fundamentalism. The immense distance of fundamentalism from theological thinking is manifest in television evangelism, an evangelism not only requiring ignorance but above all demanding deep biblical ignorance, and yet fundamentalism is now more powerful throughout the world than it has ever been, and vast numbers of people know religion only through fundamentalism. This is a truly critical situation, and for the theologian, an ultimately critical situation, and in one way or another American theologians have been engaged with this crisis for many years. This is the crisis which I once hoped to meet through what I came to think of as the Evangelical Circus. Statistically, the United States is one of the most Christian nations in history, yet many American theologians are fully persuaded that few contemporary Americans have ever encountered the Gospel, or encountered a gospel in continuity with the Bible. This is one reason for the theologian's common estrangement from the church, but another is American pietism's deep divorce from thinking and the mind, and it is pietism that is the dominant power in modern American religion.

Upon my mother's retirement she moved to Florida, and while regularly driving to visit her there I found myself hypnotized by evangelical tents for sale beside the highway, tents which had been a primary vehicle for Southern evangelism, and which came to symbolize for me a way into the deep heart of America. The mass media has become what those tents once were, and never being able to forget what Bill Hamilton had once done theologically with television—perhaps the only time that television has truly been employed theologically—I was overwhelmed by the very simple idea of employing the mass media as a vehicle for the genuine theological minds and voices of America. At that time there were many of these, or so it appeared to me, and I had met and had long conversations with dozens of them in my American odyssey. Almost all were deeply frustrated at their inability to discover a world responsive to their calling, and outraged at a public religion in America so alien to what we were persuaded was the genuine American "soul." Certainly we could meet with responses in the classroom that we could not meet in the street, so the problem presented itself of discovering a new "street," a new public square which would be the very inversion of our established one, just as we sought a true inversion of our dominant media world. This was a common motif throughout the sixties, but it had not yet been called forth theologically, or at least not called forth as a pragmatic possibility. It was that possibility that began to obsess me.

Now that I was established in the New York area this possibility seemingly became concrete. From the beginning I had been entranced by the glamorous power of the City, and recognizing that it was wholly alien to our commitment, I nevertheless thought that it had deep potentiality for us, and this had already in part been realized by Arthur Cohen and others. A concrete opportunity presented itself when I discovered the feminine religious mind of the City, women religious scholars of real power who at that time were publicly unknown, all of whom were radical in their very different ways, and in each of whom mind and voice were truly conjoined. It is very difficult to convey today the potentialities that then seemed present. Foremost among them was a potential movement from the academy to the street, and having an all too vivid sense of my hopeless inadequacies in this arena, I sought assistance and unexpectedly found it in James Morton, the dean of the Cathedral of St. John the Divine. I had gone to see him to discuss this very project, being persuaded that the cathedral had what we most needed: a magnificent site, with a superb media staff and program. Fortuitously, on the day that I saw him he was caught up in a controversy as to where the memorial service for Margaret Mead would be conducted, so his mind was very much upon the subject which I broached. And that was quite simply the employment of the cathedral as the vehicle for the first act of the Evangelical Circus, one not only centering upon the feminine religious mind, but employing it to open up for the public a new religious world.

To my deep surprise, Dean Morton gave me everything that I requested, only half-seriously requesting that we not found a new church. We could employ the cathedral on Sunday afternoons for several months, and its full staff and their radio and television broadcasting facilities would be at our service. Accordingly, our publicity problems were solved at once, to say nothing of the marvelous venue that we had been offered, and I was overjoyed. However, I had made at least one deep mistake. In the extensive conversations that I had conducted with the four women—Edith Wyschogrod, Joan Stambaugh, Elaine Pagels, and Barbara Sproul—I had always met them alone, and when we finally met together I discovered that none of them had ever met before (this could occur only in Manhattan!), so that they became far more interested in what they could do together than in my project, and to my horror they withdrew. That was the end of concrete possibilities for the Evangelical Circus, although I continued to explore them, and this was taken seriously not only by myself, but by many wiser than I am. One can only wonder what television evangelism would have become through such an Evangelical Circus, one bringing together Protestant, Catholic, Jewish, Buddhist, and atheist minds, and voices from the African American, Asian American, and European American worlds, in addition to which we intended to employ folk music, jazz and the blues to set the pace, and to set the pace for an ecstatic celebration.

One of those whom I was counting upon for this venture was Charles Long, a true preacher, historian of religions, and black theologian; we had been graduate students together at the University of Chicago, and I was wholly unprepared when he enacted an ultimate curse upon me at the 1989 annual meeting of the American Academy of Religion. This occurred at a major reception given by the leaders of the AAR and the Society of Biblical Literature, and then, as opposed to today, these leaders were heavyweights rather than lightweights. All of us were deeply shocked when suddenly, Chuck, in a drunken rage, began chanting in what was apparently an African language, directing these chants at me with a furious glare. He later explained that these chants were an ultimate curse that never could be undone. Afterwards Chuck and I and Ray Hart engaged in a long and heated conversation in Ray's hotel room, and I learned that the curse had been given because I had refused to offer the sustenance that Chuck had once so needed, a sustenance that only a fellow Southerner could offer, and when I replied that I was then so depressed and withdrawn that I could offer no one assistance, he replied with justice that this was no excuse.

After a disastrous first marriage, at that time I thought that I was happily married. My wife, Alma, a brilliant and beautiful woman, is deeply religious and she was fully being drawn into a pagan theology and praxis, or into what today is known as a New Age spirituality. This was creating deep tensions between us, but tensions that I was persuaded could be resolved. Yet when I returned to Long Island after that curse, Alma almost immediately left me, even leaving the children largely in my care, and for a reason that was wholly inexplicable to me. Soon I was engaged in a deep conversation with Mircea Eliade about this. Mircea was very close to Chuck, and he not only understood "magic" as no one else did, but he had no doubt of its contemporary reality, as fully manifest in his fiction. It was Mircea who first suggested to me that it was Chuck's curse that had ended my marriage, and both Mircea and his wife, Christenel, were close to Alma. Of course, this is not to relieve me of responsibility here, but this disaster for me is an apt paradigm of what for the theologian is the full integration of understanding and praxis. There is nothing that we can genuinely understand theologically that does not have a real impact upon us, and even if a disastrous impact, as it commonly is; religious or theological understanding is wholly unreal if it is removed from praxis, or removed from an ultimate and overwhelming impact upon us.

Hence I was persuaded that it is not possible to be a genuine theologian without being open to a radical judgment, or to damnation itself, nor could I easily teach radical theology. I almost never employed my own books as classroom texts, and my one attempt to publish a textbook of radical theology culminated with virtually no sales. Yet I had no doubt of the deep potential power of radical theology in our world, and I could even see this power as becoming universal in our new world. Most of us theologians were then absorbing that power from a seemingly secular world, and just as the theologian could discover a deep theological power in the philosophical thinking of a Hegel, a Nietzsche, a Whitehead, a Heidegger, or a Wittgenstein, everyone can be open to its power in our literature and art, or even in our history itself. My book on Eliade had attempted to demonstrate that it is his theological thinking which is the real source of his power as a historian of religions. While this alienated most of his followers who were establishing their own credentials as nontheological historians of religions, it certainly never alienated Mircea himself, and while I believe that he played a major role in the genesis of the American death of God theology, that role continues to baffle me. This problem becomes most concrete for me in what I regard as his most perplexing public statement, and that is when he declares that the theology of "the death of God" is extremely important because it is the sole religious creation of the modern Western world (*Mircea Eliade: Ordeal by Labyrinth*, Chicago: University of Chicago Press, 1982, p. 151). What could he possibly mean by this? He is certainly not simply referring to my theology, which was the only death of God theology that he knew, nor do I believe that he was referring to anything that we commonly think of as theology, but rather to a uniquely modern vision in which there is a full and total *coincidentia oppositorum* of the sacred and the profane.

It was through Eliade that I had my deepest sense of religious calling, one that culminated in what I believe was a genuine initiation, but which I can now recount as though it were only a dream, and a dream of a contemporary shamanic initiation. Not long before his death I had come to Chicago to give a lecture at a philosophical conference at Northwestern, and we had planned that I would have a long session with Eliade on the Saturday following this. But on that early Saturday morning I found myself stranded on the South side after a long evening with a faculty friend at the University of Chicago. No public transportation was available to take me to my hotel room in Evanston, and suddenly in a deserted street I was visited by a strange company of eerie figures dancing about me and beckoning me to accompany them. This I did, and even ecstatically so, to what destination I cannot remember, but when I did wake up the next morning I was on the floor of a graduate student's room where I had been taken for recovery. Slowly I made my way to the Eliades' apartment, and Mircea immediately greeted me with the inquiry as to whether I had been well cared for by the "ghosts." This was no light question from one who so deeply believed in them, for ghosts are the spirits of those dead who never leave us, and I realized that these ghosts were instruments of Mircea's, and instruments of my initiation.

This occurred over the following two hours, and I was given a truly new sense of mission. That initiation entailed a deep bonding with Mircea, one in which I could name him as my father, and when I was later greeted by Christenel, I could respond to her as "mother." If only now, I deeply knew that I was not alone, that there truly is a communion of the saints, and the saints are everyone, or everyone who is alive, but here life is life only through death, and while every student of religion knows that ultimately life is only possible through death, now I knew that I had actually been initiated into this, and thus openly initiated into my own vocation. Mircea knew my vocation more deeply than anyone else whom I knew, and he had recognized it almost at once, and as a genuine master he had always allowed me to find my own way. It was only all too gradually that I realized that my way was not ultimately different from his, and this realization occurred most concretely in this initiation. Thus I believe that there are ways in which I have been his surrogate, and not only his but the surrogate of many others as well, for theology is truly a communal enterprise, thereby deeply differing from both poetry and philosophy, and as a communal project it is directed to a public or universal world, and this in a way that has become impossible for both our philosophy and our poetry.

Another initiation was given me in Seoul, Korea, and this one truly strange. I had been there one summer as a visiting professor at Ewha University, and once again I was continually on television, largely because a repressive political situation gave few opportunities for their mass media, and they seemed to be delighted to discover in me an innocuous surrogate. This did bring me a certain public attention, and shortly before I was to leave a major political figure contacted me with an invitation to visit a new Korean cult, an apocalyptic one, and one apparently open to my own thinking (I was known there as a Buddhist-Christian theologian). When I arrived with a close friend, David Suh, who would act as my interpreter, I was immediately taken to their master, who turned out to be a middle-aged Korean housewife, with no advanced education but who some time ago had suddenly begun to chant in exotic languages, languages that had been discovered to be Sanskrit and Chinese, and when recorded and transcribed they turned out to be full versions of the Buddhist scriptures. Following this, a new revelation occurred, this time in Korean, and a fully apocalyptic revelation announcing the immediate advent of a universal apocalypse. She greeted me with a deep bow, and while this is common in the Far East, this one clearly had a special meaning, which became concrete when she announced to her followers that she had already called me two thousand years ago, then naming me as Paul. My mission was then to bring the Buddha to the West, and my mission now was to be her instrument in opening the world to a universal epiphany of the Buddha. She herself, she confided to me, was the apocalyptic Buddha.

Clearly her followers took her with deep seriousness, and they seemed to comprise a Korean elite. By this time the world knew of an apocalyptic Korea if only through Sun Moon, but this was a Buddhist as opposed to a Christian apocalypticism, although each are universal in their scope. This Buddha commanded me to fly to San Francisco immediately, there to publicly announce the imminence of the final coming of the Buddha, whence I was to proceed to Washington where I was to preside over their new world center, for we would soon be overwhelmed by millions if not billions of eager seekers. Needless to say I betrayed this command. Perhaps I have betrayed every genuine command, and if this was a comic rather than a genuine command, it is not without a deep irony, or deep irony for me, because I believe that theology itself now has some such vocation, and this belief has deepened as my vocation has evolved. Of course, we have been flooded with counterfeit ecumenical theologies, and ecumenical cults of every possible kind, but if nothing else these demonstrate the hunger that now is present, a hunger ruthlessly denied or evaded by our church theologies, with the all too significant exception of the Roman Catholic world.

No more revolutionary theological event has occurred in the twentieth century than the Second Vatican Council, one truly reversing the

First Vatican Council of the nineteenth century. Now the Catholic Church has actually entered the modern world, but as Eastern Orthodox theologians know so deeply, it was the Catholic Church that ultimately created the modern Western world, and did so through what the Eastern Christian can recognize as a truly atheistic theology. I shall never forget that when I was introduced as an atheistic theologian to the Russian poet, Joseph Brodsky, he immediately said that of course I was, since all Western theologians are so. The truly contemporary Catholic theologian has not only unveiled the God of modern scholasticism as an empty and alien God, but demonstrated what a deep betrayal this is of an authentic Catholic tradition. Here an anti-Catholicism is seemingly far deeper than it is in the Protestant world, but this very "anti-Catholicism" can be understood as a deep Catholicism, and one genuine continuity with its deepest Catholic roots, so that for the first time in the modern world we are witnessing the birth of a Catholic theology that is a biblical theology, and just thereby a deeply contemporary theology as well. Already Tillich recognized that a new Catholicism is ending the historical role of Protestantism, hence Tillich sought to bring together Catholic substance with the Protestant principle, but this has already occurred in a new Catholic theology, and one which promised to be most radical in America itself.

Clearly this has not yet fully occurred, or not yet openly or publicly occurred, but it may be occurring nonetheless, and just as I have received genuine support from the Catholic world, this could be said of all of our theological radicals, who have frequently been inspired by a deep Catholic radicalism. That Catholic theological radicalism is commonly unknown in the secular world is simply a scandal, but it is certainly not unknown in the Vatican, and it is of great significance that the known intention of the Vatican to reign in contemporary Catholic theology and higher education is simply impossible to execute. Nowhere is this truer than in America, and if America is the center of a new Catholic wealth and power, it is not one that can finally be intimidated by the Vatican, or by any ecclesiastical power. Yet this is most true in our imaginative and intellectual worlds, and just as the deep transformation of the American Catholic university world since the Second World War is seemingly miraculous, there has simultaneously occurred a deep transformation of the American Catholic mind, and nowhere is this more fully embodied than in D. G.

Leahy. I first met Leahy when he came to my office at Stony Brook seeking a job, a job that I was in no position to give him. He left in my hands a manuscript entitled "Novitas Mundi," and while this appeared to be and is in fact forbidding, there was something about his presence and voice that captivated me, and that night, when I was once again visited by insomnia, I arose and for some strange reason began reading "Novitas Mundi." I have never been the same again.

That reading was something like a conversion, or the occurrence of a deep calling—one seeming to have little to do with my previous calling, but this is untrue, for Leahy is a profoundly theological thinker, even if he is a thinker who is philosophical and theological at once. Moreover, his thinking intends to be the most revolutionary thinking in history, and it is a genuine apocalyptic thinking, the fullest and purest apocalyptic thinking that we have been given. While these motifs are only openly present in *Novitas Mundi* in its three appendices, these appendices incorporate the most original and radical thinking in the book, and it is these which most decisively open the way to his next book, *Foundation: Matter the Body Itself.* This is a book containing long excursions into my own theology, excursions transcending my own in terms of their sheer power, and even if they reveal my theology as a "black mass," they reveal it as nothing else does, and therefore I can only greet them with celebration. But what can one say about David Leahy as a human being? Who is this one who more deeply than anyone else in the West has unthought selfhood itself, and more deeply and comprehensively than anyone else not only called forth but actually thought an absolutely new world, and thought it in that "thinking now occurring for the first time" that appears through the name of D. G. Leahy? Is this the name of anyone at all?

Perhaps someday I shall only be known as the one who discovered Leahy, or first brought him public attention, but it was only through years of intense reading and thinking that I could truly become open to Leahy, and while I saw a great deal of him during those years, and was constantly trying in vain to help him secure a genuine academic position, I only knew him as a deep mystery, for this is one who is not only a pure thinker, but one whom I believe is perhaps a saint as well. It has been a very long time since we have known holy thinkers. The mere fact that so many of his followers know Heidegger as both a holy and a revelatory thinker is scandalous in itself, but the deep thinker has always been known as a holy thinker in the East, and this has been true in the West in Neoplatonism, our longest continuous philosophical tradition. Leahy would reverse Neoplatonism, as every radical Catholic thinker has done, and while this is only partially accomplished by Augustine and Aquinas, it occurs fully and totally in Leahy, who if only thereby stands forth as a profound Catholic thinker, and above all so in his pure and total thinking of body itself. Here, deep body is a truly holy body, the Body of the Eucharist itself, but it is precisely thereby an apocalyptic body that is the body of an absolutely new universe, and yet a body which is now pure thinking itself. I think that it is simply undeniable that this is a genuinely Catholic thinking, but a Catholic thinking that is a universal thinking, and therefore one fully unveiling the truly revolutionary ground of Catholicism itself.

Once this is accepted, then revolutionary thinking itself acquires a new meaning, for if throughout modernity Catholic thinking is our most reactionary thinking, it is now apparently reversing itself, and just thereby becoming a more truly Catholic thinking, and not only Catholic in its new universal horizon, but Catholic in its centering upon body and world, and if a new natural theology and a new revelatory theology are now not only inseparable but also indistinguishable, then a truly if not absolutely new Catholicism may well have arrived. This was certainly a deep hope of many of my Catholic friends and associates, and it is fascinating to me that today it is apparently only in Catholic circles that genuine hope survives, and if ours is the most conservative world in full modernity, and one in which every real hope can seemingly only appear and be real as fantasy, it is Catholicism, the most truly fantastic world of modernity itself, one giving us our purest and most comprehensive illusions, that now is giving us a real hope, one that has wholly perished in Protestantism, or can survive in Protestantism only in its most sectarian and otherworldly expressions. Perhaps nowhere else is the deep irony of history so clearly manifest today, but it is also ironic that we should simultaneously know such a universal secularity and such a comprehensive religiosity, and if this is truly foreshadowed in the Roman Empire and the Hellenistic world, it is the Catholic Church that is the embodiment of that world; and if imperialism has become universal in the modern world as it never did in the ancient world, such a process may be occurring religiously today, but if so it can occur only by way of a deep and universal religious revolution.

The fact is that religious revolutions have occurred many times in our past, and if the axial revolution that occurred between the eighth and the fourth centuries BCE is the deepest revolution that has ever occurred, and also our most universal revolution—for it occurred in Greece, Israel, India, and China virtually simultaneously—this is clearly a religious revolution, even if it comprehensively occurred throughout consciousness and society. There are scholars who believe that the very word "religion" is a deep betrayal of that which it seemingly evokes, and that as a word and concept it became fully meaningful only with the full advent of a deeply secular world, and above all so in its dualistic division between the religious and the secular or the sacred and the profane, but it cannot be denied that this is a deep motif of ancient Christian theological thinking, even if alien to the Bible itself. Many if not most of us theologians were attempting to think through this very division after the Second World War, and Barth had created modern dialectical theology by positing an absolute dichotomy between religion and faith. At no other point has Barth been more influential, just as at no other point did he seem to betray himself more deeply than in embarking upon his *Church Dogmatics*. So at this time in America Tillich was more influential than Barth in the theological world as a whole, and although Tillich as opposed to Barth never succeeded in establishing a theological school, he had a deep impact, indeed, and perhaps most so in the birth of a uniquely American atheistic theology. At no other point has American theology been so unique, but this I believe is the reflection of a uniquely American experience, one truly embodied in our deeper literature, and one which we intended to evoke at a conference at Emory on America and the future of theology. I was often ridiculed because the influences upon me were clearly more European than American, but Leahy is not irresponsible in looking upon my theology as a culmination of a uniquely American thinking, and if Ray Hart could inspire me with the wilderness tradition in America, I have ever regarded *Moby-Dick* as the deepest American epic, just as I came to believe that the death of God first enters full and comprehensive historical actuality in America. It was H. L. Mencken's great book on the American language that allowed me to see that this fully occurs in our language itself, and above all so in its obliteration or reversal of all distinctions between high and low. Nothing is more unique in American poetry than its deep atheistic ground, and if this drove Eliot to Europe, it was the Christian and American Eliot who created a *coincidentia oppositorum* between the sacred and the profane in *Four Quartets*, and one that is already present in *The Waste Land*. I remember Eliot remarking at the University of Chicago that the Church of England had succeeded in inoculating the English against Christianity, and I must confess that England has long appeared to me as the most profane of nations, and the one which has most succeeded in betraying its own religious revolution. But did a religious revolution ever occur in America? Surely the first separation between church and state is less than that, or is it? Is it this separation which is a deep ground of a uniquely American atheism or secularism, and one which can be most deeply religious in that very separation, or even in a truly new dichotomy between the religious and the secular or the sacred and the profane?

Such questions are still being debated, but all passion now seems absent from our debates, as witness not only our political but our religious world. Theology once thrived in passionate debate, debate so passionate that it could culminate in torture and execution, but now our debates are civil, indeed, so civil as to be passionless, as though they could not possibly have a deep effect. But if they cannot have a deep effect they cannot be deeply important, and perhaps nothing is deeply important today, or so it would appear, unless this very absence is truly important. The overwhelming difference between our academic meetings today and those of a generation ago is significant. We then knew intense debates lasting throughout the night, and these made possible a deep and intimate meeting, just as they called forth genuine rancor and controversy, and if that now seems like a vanished world, has there also vanished any hope or expectation that thinking and the imagination can deeply and actually affect the world? Is religious revolution only an academic category, one of interest only in a purely academic inquiry, or, is it, in fact, occurring in the world, and in our world, even if only occurring invisibly?

CHAPTER 5

Holocaust

An extraordinarily difficult question facing those of us who are committed to a new theology is quite simply the question of language and style. How do we think and write in that new language which is now demanded? Is this even an actual possibility for us? It was with Mark Taylor that I seemed to share this question most fully. At his invitation I spent a year as a visiting professor at Williams College, and it was then that we most deeply shared our work. Many theologians have pointed to Taylor as one who has clearly abandoned theology, as is evident in the common theological response to his *Erring*, but then and now I judge this to be a genuinely theological work, and it is most creative precisely in its new language. While there is much here that is deeply alien to me, there is much that I also genuinely share, and while I cannot share his later focus upon virtual reality, I can see the necessity of a comparable transmutation of my own work, one that to some extent has already occurred. It was at Williams that I completed the chapter on Joyce in *History as Apocalypse*. I continue to believe that the language of *Finnegans Wake* is the fullest embodiment of a new theological language, and nothing has more gratified me in response to my writing than when Norman O. Brown wrote me that here at last the theology of the Wake had been understood. Recognizing, however, that I am not and cannot be a full writer, I have been forced into partial resolutions, resolutions not only calling upon the reader to enact what is read, but accepting this very limitation as a necessity for genuine theology, which unlike poetry and philosophy cannot be the product of a single creator, and is itself only truly theological in a fully communal context and world.

Of course, a real problem is just what is that world in which theology is now spoken; I join innumerable theologians in believing that this can no longer be only a church or a religious institution, and never before has there been a deeper chasm between religious institutions and the world, thus foreclosing the possibility of a church theology that could be a theology for the world, or a church theology that could be anything but a sectarian theology. Catholicism may finally be an exception to this, but not in the foreseeable future, or in any future in genuine continuity with our world. The paradigm that I have chosen for meeting this problem derives from my understanding of the Christian epic tradition, a tradition in which the Christian vision itself is profoundly transformed, and transformed by a purely inner evolution, one truly incarnational and truly apocalyptic at once; indeed, it is an ultimate apocalyptic movement that is inescapably an incarnational movement, a movement that we now know was most distinctive of an original Christianity and of Jesus himself. Nothing more shocks me about New Testament scholarship than its dominant judgment that both Jesus and primitive Christianity were truly and deeply apocalyptic with its common corollary that apocalypticism is truly alien to our world. More accurately stated, apocalypticism is truly alien to our dominant religious world, whereas it is truly central in the deepest or most radical expressions of our political, our conceptual, and our imaginative life, as witness not only the Christian epic, but modern dialectical thinking itself, which has been profoundly apocalyptic, whether implicitly or explicitly, in Hegel, Kierkegaard, Marx, and Nietzsche.

True, both Blake and Joyce are profoundly heterodox, but Dante and Milton were deeply heterodox in their own worlds, and if it is possible to see that the visions of Joyce and Blake evolved out of the visions of Milton and Dante, and if this evolution is a truly apocalyptic evolution, then we are here given a way into a truly new theological language, and a new theological language which could be a rebirth or renewal of biblical language, as certainly occurs in Dante and Milton, and which also occurs in Blake and Joyce. Indeed, if only through the Christian epic we can sense the possibility of a systematic theology going vastly beyond anything previously known as systematic theology, and just as the *Commedia* is far more comprehensive than the *Summa Theologica*, and *Paradise Lost* truly more comprehensive than

any Protestant dogmatics, the possibilities have been established for us
of a truly comprehensive theology, and one that is already present in
the epic visions of Blake and Joyce. This is a calling going far beyond
the power of this theologian, but it is a calling that could be exercised
communally, and if theology truly is a communal activity, and one
directed to the whole world upon its horizon, then such a calling if not
being truly exercised today, may nevertheless be arising or aborning in
our world, and even if this is an invisible birthing, it could nevertheless be actual and real.

Such at least has been my deep hope, and I have long sought an
apparently nontheological reader or hearer, believing that theology is a
truly universal calling, and just as it often occurs where it is least
apparent, here the theologian incurs a deep debt. Debt in its depth is
overtly theological, and if our deepest debt is to "God," this very debt
is inexplicable today as it has never previously been; yet we can know
deep debt as a deep gift, and a deep gift making inexplicably possible
an ultimate life. Here, genesis itself becomes an overwhelming problem, and I became possessed by the theological problem of understanding true genesis as an apocalyptic genesis, as the actual advent of
an absolutely new world, but a new world occurring only through an
apocalyptic death, an apocalyptic death which is absolute genesis
itself. This is the problem broached by *Genesis and Apocalypse*, a
book seeking a new theological language, but a new theological language which is an apocalyptic language, and thus a language directed
against all existing theological languages, or all existing manifest theological languages, which are clearly non-apocalyptic languages and
hence alienated from the prophetic and apocalyptic languages of the
Bible. Here, I was under a real debt to recent biblical scholarship,
which has shattered every given theological distinction between the
eschatological and the apocalyptic, and thereby shattered every biblical claim of all established Christian theology.

Of course, *Genesis and Apocalypse* is also deeply indebted to
Buddhism, and while the Buddhologist can truly know this book as an
irresponsible exegesis of Buddhism, a Buddhist horizon makes possible this apocalyptic understanding, and above all so a Buddhist understanding of an absolute nothingness or an absolute void, apart from
which apocalypse itself is a meaningless surd, which is at least one
reason why theologians have been unable to understand apocalypse.

But so, too, has an absolute nothingness been an ultimate ground of modernity itself, as fully manifest in our deepest modern poetry, and even in truly crucial expressions of our deepest modern thinking. This is true not only of Hegel, Schelling, Nietzsche, and Heidegger, but of Kierkegaard, too, and even of that Kierkegaard who has had the deepest impact upon modern theology. This is the very point at which the Kyoto School has been able to create a truly ecumenical Buddhist philosophy, one drawing forth a uniquely Western absolute nothingness as a decisive way into a uniquely Buddhist absolute nothingness, so that here an Eckhart, a Hegel, a Nietzsche, a Heidegger, and even a Kirkegaard, can truly be ways into Buddhism, and into a universal Buddhism. Note that here Buddhist thinking is far more universal than any form of Christian thinking, and it can take as its ground a uniquely modern *Angst*, or a uniquely modern nothingness, allowing that very ground to open to the depths of a uniquely Buddhist apocalypse.

Certainly I was profoundly affected by these Buddhist thinkers. Here is a pure theology, and a pure theology that is a universal theology, even employing the death of God in the Crucifixion as a way to a uniquely Buddhist Emptiness, and this was the very point at which the deepest dialogue occurred between my Buddhist friends and myself. Yes, I have attempted to evolve a Buddhist Christian theology, but this was previously accomplished by Nishida and the Kyoto School, and there are ways in which my theology is a reflection of theirs, just as it is also a reflection, even if a pale one, of our deepest Western visions of an absolute nothingness. Nihilism itself realizes a truly new meaning here, and even a truly holy meaning, and just as an apophatic mysticism can know Godhead itself as an absolute nothingness, and therefore know an absolute nothingness as an absolutely holy nothingness, our deepest modern visionaries have called forth an absolute nothingness which is a holy nothingness, and holy precisely as that nothingness itself. At no other point is there a deeper coincidence between the ancient and the modern, or between the sacred and the profane, and even if full modernity is an absolute reversal of a sacred totality, it is that modernity only by way of this reversal, and therefore only by way of what is symbolically called forth as the death of God. Yes, the death of God is by necessity a renewal or resurrection of an absolute nothingness, thus nihilism inevitably follows in its wake, but now and for the first time nihilism is established as a universal horizon, and one which is actually known by everyone who is now awake.

Nihilism has been most actual and concrete for us in the Holocaust, and it was by calling forth the Holocaust as an irrefutable witness to the death of God that Richard Rubenstein had an overwhelming impact as a radical Jewish theologian. Rubenstein did not hesitate to insist that any genuine understanding of providence must now accept the Holocaust as occurring within the providence of God. This is just why he rejected any and every theistic God, and sought a holy nothingness that can only be found within a primordial horizon. Is this just the point at which there is an uncrossable gulf between a primordial horizon and our contemporary horizon, or is a holy nothingness present in our world, and even in the depths of our nihilism itself? The Holocaust is an inescapable challenge here, and if we can know it as the most horrible historical event that has ever occurred, is it just thereby a refutation of any possible providence, or of any possible providence in our world? And is the Holocaust itself a decisive witness to what we can only know as a full epiphany of Satan, a full embodiment of an absolute evil, and an absolute evil that is here truly incarnate? How is it possible that in the wake of the Holocaust there has been virtually no theological naming of Satan? Is this because our deepest voice has been stilled, has been numbed into a truly new passivity and impotence?

Ever increasingly I became convinced that if we cannot actually name Satan then we cannot actually name Christ. This is a dialectical naming that not only deeply occurs in the New Testament, but is unique to the New Testament, except insofar as it is reborn in a uniquely Christian vision, and here, too, the Christian epic tradition is in deeper continuity with the New Testament than any other writing that we have been given. Indeed, Blake's epic vision culminates in a *coincidentia oppositorum* between Christ and Satan, yet Blake's Satan is the absolutely alien or absolutely fallen Creator, that very Creator who is the absolute sovereignty of God, and who is truly the Lord of a totally fallen history. Here, one can know the Holocaust as the consequence of the providence of "God," but for the mature Blake pure evil is an absolutely atoning evil, one inseparable from what he knew as the "Self Annihilation" of God, and a self-annihilation occurring most deeply in the passion and death of Christ. So far as I know I am the only theologian who has attempted a theological incorporation of Blake's vision, and this is just the point at which this is most difficult and most challenging: Can we understand the actuality of absolute evil as inevitably being an atoning process, or is this far too blasphemous a possibility to contemplate? Yet is it possible to be open to the Holocaust and to refuse this question? Or is the only possible response quite simply silence itself?

The truth is that our philosophy has always responded to evil with a deep silence, one which is not broken until Kant, Hegel, Schelling, and Nietzsche. Although such a silence has been renewed in the philosophical thinking of the twentieth century, so likewise our theology has finally known evil as nothingness itself, and not an absolute nothingness but rather a pure and simple nothingness, a nothingness which is the privation of the good. Is it possible to know the Holocaust as such a nothingness? Surely this would be a truly blasphemous response, for it would be a denial of the absolute evil of the Holocaust, and thereby a denial of absolute evil itself, and if we cannot know an absolute evil, how could we possibly know the Holocaust itself? Yet we cannot know an absolute evil without naming "Satan," and we must recall that an actual naming of Satan did not occur until the advent of apocalypticism, and just as an apocalyptic naming of Satan has always been our deepest naming of Satan, this does not come to an end with the advent of the modern world. It far rather deepens with that very advent, as witness Milton, nor does it come to an end in late modernity, as witness Joyce. All too significantly, *Finnegans Wake* was completed just before the Holocaust occurred, and while the *Wake* is our most comprehensive drawing forth of Satan, it ends with a total and an apocalyptic Yes, and with an apocalypse that can be understood as a *coincidentia oppositorum* of Christ and Satan. Is this not a way into the Holocaust itself?

One of my deep friends with whom I most deeply discussed the theological meaning of the Holocaust is Edith Wyschogrod. While Edith is professionally a philosopher, she is a theologian, too, and her philosophical work has never been truly isolated from her theological thinking, as witness her long immersion in and even identification with Levinas, that one major twentieth-century philosopher who has actually thought about God or the Infinite, and whose thinking about God is a deeply Jewish or aniconic thinking, and one which Edith has extended into truly new arenas in her understanding of alterity. I think that this understanding is only possible by way of the Holocaust. Certainly no other American thinker has thought more purely about the Holocaust; one almost senses that apart from the Holocaust she could not truly think. And is it truly possible in our world actually to think about God without thinking of the Holocaust? There are those who think or suspect that it is the Holocaust which has finally made possible an unthinking of God, but this is certainly not true of either Levinas or Wyschogrod. It is far rather that the Holocaust has here finally made possible a thinking of the absolute alterity of God, and it cannot be denied that it was either a pre-Holocaust or a post-Holocaust situation which made possible our deepest fully modern Jewish thinking. I have encountered that thinking in deep friends such as Walter Strauss and Arthur Cohen, and this very thinking is overwhelming in its sheer power. For the first time Jewish thinking has become a virtually universal thinking through the impact of Buber, Levinas, and Derrida, and while this thinking can be understood as an inversion of Christian theological thinking, that is surely at least one source of its very power as thinking. Levinas is the only twentieth-century philosopher who has written seriously about evil, and that fact itself is important. Is it only the Holocaust that makes possible for us a genuine thinking about evil, and is our very impotence in thinking about evil a decisive sign of our deep passivity, a passivity which our first great modern Jewish thinker, Spinoza, could know even if he could not name it as pure evil, and a passivity which seemed to possess the German people at the time of the Holocaust? Oddly enough, it was during this period that I first began seriously thinking about Spinoza; I wonder if it was wrestling with the Holocaust that made this possible, and it is above all Spinoza's understanding of God which would appear here to be a decisive key, a God whose very totality comprehends everything whatsoever, and yet a God who is pure action or pure activity, an absolute necessity which is the source of all and everything. Spinoza claimed to forswear all thinking about evil, but he nevertheless thought about evil in thinking a pure passivity, and if that passivity must inevitably here be understood as the very opposite of God, it is nonetheless one that possesses the great majority of humanity. Indeed, Spinoza could even understand passivity itself as the very source of every philosophical understanding of teleology or final causation. Spinoza was the first philosophical thinker who unthought that teleology, one inseparable from his negation or dissolution of subject or interiority, and this very dissolution was an ultimate philosophical thinking of God, and as such the first philosophical negation or deconstruction of what Heidegger came to understand as ontotheology.

This was accomplished far more purely by Spinoza than by Heidegger. Perhaps it is only possible for the Jewish thinker, hence it is reborn in both Levinas and Derrida, but now reborn in response to the Holocaust, and one can never lose sight of the Holocaust in reading either Levinas or Derrida, just as we also should never lose sight of it in reading any theology today. Is it only through the Holocaust that we can know the true alterity of God, and is that an alterity truly different from what Christian theology has traditionally known as the pure transcendence of God? An alterity that cannot be known as Christian theology has known transcendence, and cannot be so known if only because here it is not possible truly to know God at all? There is certainly a deep aniconic ground in the Jew which is alien to the Christian, a ground precluding any possibility of incarnation, and just as the Jewish Messiah is deeply different from the Christian Messiah, a Messiah who could never be the Son of God, the Jewish apocalypse is radically different from the Christian apocalypse, and is so if only because it could never actually be envisioned, and all too significantly rabbinic Judaism was only truly born with a full negation of apocalyptic Judaism.

Nevertheless, the Jew can respond to the Holocaust as an apocalyptic event, but it is an apocalypse of absolute evil, or what the Christian must inevitably identify as a Satanic apocalypse, and just as it is only the Christian who can know the Jew as the murderer of God, and who for two millennia did know the Jew as the murderer of God, so the Christian must know the Holocaust as a Satanic apocalypse only made possible by Christianity. Every Jew knows this, and every Christian should know it, but that must finally mean that it is the Christian God who is a deep source of the Holocaust, and the uniquely Christian God, a God known to the Christian alone, that God whom both

Kierkegaard and Nietzsche could know as an absolute No-saying, and that God whom Blake could name as Satan. Now even if the conservative theologian would respond by affirming that it is only the Christian Gnostic who can know God as Satan, no one has been so deeply anti-Gnostic as are Blake and Nietzsche. Barth himself, in what is perhaps the deepest section of *Church Dogmatics* (II, 2) has affirmed that the specific service for which Israel is determined by God is to reflect the judgment from which God has rescued man, and over against the witness of the church it can set forth only the sheer, stark judgment of God, only the obduracy and consequent misery of man, only the sentence and punishment that God in His mercy has chosen to undergo Himself. The church stands in the same relation to Israel as does the Resurrection of Jesus to his Crucifixion, as God's mercy to His judgment. This section of Barth's dogmatics was written at the very time that the Holocaust was occurring, and while Barth himself was a genuine and active anti-Nazi, we can see even in his deepest theology a Christian ground for the Holocaust itself.

Indeed, Barth's famous calling forth of that ultimate sin which is manifest in the betrayal of Judas Iscariot (II, 2, 35, 4) largely revolves about a portrait of the betrayal of Israel. It is here that Barth most fully portrays Satan, and here that we learn that Judas does what Israel has always done in relation to Yahweh, for Israel always tried to buy off Yahweh with thirty pieces of silver, and Judas is not only all Israel, but in and with him the Jews as such! The end of Judaism occurred when Judas handed Jesus over, and with the killing of the Messiah, Israel entered a road on which not only is God's judgment upon its whole existence inevitable, "but in sheer self-consistency it must end by committing suicide" (page 470), and while this occurred in its revolt against the Romans, this is a death which is not an expiation for its sins but only their consummation. Barth then affirms, in this volume on election or predestination, that in the New Testament the divine determination of the damned or rejected is unambiguously clear, and especially in the person and act of Judas. Yet Barth is finally the radical Barth, and is so here by affirming that Judas is the "holy" apostle, "holy" in the old meaning of the term, one who is cursed, and the elect always occupy the place that was originally occupied by the rejected. And God in His burning wrath does to men what Judas did to Jesus. He takes their freedom from them and makes them totally powerless, just as God Himself is the One who hands over Jesus, and it was the divine omnipotence of which Jesus let himself be robbed, and did so by means of Judas. Nevertheless, Judas, in his concentrated attack upon Israel's Messiah, does only what the elect people of Israel had always done towards its God, and in Judas there lives again all the great rejected of the Old Testament, a people who are elected in and from its rejection, and in view of the act of Judas there can be no further doubt about the rejection of this people, and the rejection of all those individuals within it. Yet Jesus Christ also dies for rejected Israel, and therefore even rejected Israel is always in the open, and the question of its future can never be put except in this situation.

Barth's theology is the most influential theology of the twentieth century, and while no one would lay the Holocaust upon Barth's hands, how could one deny that it is just this kind of thinking that could open the possibility of the Holocaust? There are orthodox Jewish theologians who maintain that the Holocaust was God's just judgment upon the Jew's modern apostasy, but there are few if any Christian theologians who now affirm that the Holocaust occurred through the providence of God, and this despite the fact that orthodox theology has always affirmed that God is finally the source of every event, a denial of which would be a denial of the absolute sovereignty of God. I was a theologian who was in process of becoming a full theologian of predestination. It was while I was struggling with the theological challenge of the Holocaust that I began most fully to understand predestination, and just as in classical Western theology predestination is a double predestination, a simultaneous predestination to Heaven and to Hell, I came to understand providence itself as a double predestination, and one eternally willed by God. This is most clearly manifest in the Holocaust if the Holocaust is finally an atoning event, and the Christian has come to look upon the martyrs of the Holocaust as holy or atoning martyrs, martyrs repeating or renewing the Crucifixion itself. Then just as the Crucifixion can be known by the Christian as that ultimate victory of Satan which is finally the apocalyptic ending of Satan, the Holocaust could be understood as a comparable event, although now an apocalyptic ending is the ending of our world. But how to speak of this in and to a world which had lost all sense of damnation and Satan, and paradoxically so given the Holocaust itself? Even Barth is all too muted in speaking of Satan and

Hell, and while he deeply affirms that because of the Crucifixion damnation has become "objectively" impossible for all, this is the one point at which he clearly abandons a traditional Protestant dogmatics, and abandons ancient Christianity as well. How is that possible for an orthodox theologian, or possible for that Barth who knows the absolute judgment of God more deeply than any other theologian since Augustine, or that dialectical Barth who knows God's Yes only through God's No? Is this not a profound inconsistency? While Barth does affirm that there does exist a definite sphere of damnation ordained by God as the negation of the divine affirmation, that is the work of "the almighty non-willing" which accompanies God's willing, for if Jesus Christ is the very Yes of God, that Yes cannot be heard unless the No of God is also heard, but that No is said for the sake of the Yes, and therefore the first and last word of God is Yes and not No. Nevertheless, the No of God is inseparable from the Yes of God, or inseparable for us, and surely we can hear the No of God in the Holocaust itself, for to refuse that No would be to refuse the Holocaust, or to refuse the Holocaust as the embodiment of an absolute evil, and hence one which we can only hear as the No of God.

How is it possible for the Christian to speak of an absolute evil without speaking of God? This would be to succumb to a Manichean or Gnostic temptation, one that has ever tempted the Christian theologian, and perhaps never more so than today. Augustine established the deepest foundations of Western theology by overcoming that temptation, and if it was Augustine who established the very dogma of predestination, that dogma is inseparable from everything that he most deeply understood as freedom and grace, and just as Augustine was the philosophical discoverer of the freedom of the will, that is a discovery inseparable from a discovery of the absolute impotence of the will, one that can only be broken by the grace of God, and by that grace of God which is the grace of predestination. Augustine was the first theologian after Paul to know that the absolute Yes and the absolute No of God are inseparable. It is this simultaneity that is most deeply called forth by the dogma of predestination, so that eternal redemption and eternal damnation are inseparable, and this is a simultaneity even interiorly known by us when we simultaneously know the freedom and the impotence of the will. Augustine has ever been my deepest theological master, and once I realized that it was impossible to be an Augustinian theologian without being a theologian of predestination, I also realized that redemption is wholly unreal apart from damnation, and just as Barth could know the "rejection" or damnation of Christ as the source of redemption, an understanding which is his understanding of election or predestination, I became persuaded that it is only in knowing the depths of darkness or damnation that we can know redemption, and that darkness is nowhere more manifest to us than in the Holocaust.

Perhaps the supreme theological problem is the problem or mystery of the meaning of an ultimate and absolute Yes. If this is the very center of every genuine faith, it has never been so obscure and precarious as it is today, and this despite the fact that the enactment of such a Yes is so absolutely primary in our uniquely modern visionary voyages, one that finally can occur even in its seemingly total absence, as in Kafka and Beckett, and one that remains absolutely primary in even our deepest atheism, as in Marx and Nietzsche. This is just the point at which modern theological apologetics has wholly broken down, for in full modernity an absolute Yes has been far deeper and purer in our secular worlds than in our religious worlds, and theologically it has been most powerful in that Barth who cannot pronounce the Yes of God without pronouncing the No of God. At this point Barth is in deep continuity with that Nietzsche who so totally conjoined Yes-saying and No-saying, and if Nietzsche's vision of Eternal Recurrence is a uniquely modern vision of predestination, as I attempt to demonstrate in *Genesis and Apocalypse*, no thinker has ever pronounced an absolute Yes more totally than did Nietzsche, but this is a Yes that can only be willed or enacted when we will the eternal recurrence of everything that has occurred. Nietzsche did not hesitate to demand the willing of the deepest evil in the willing of eternal recurrence; only such a willing could be the willing of actuality itself, and unlike an ancient *amor fati*, this is not a passive acceptance of the world but a willing of the deepest actuality of the world itself. That is the very will which is absolute Will itself or the Will to Power, or that will which Augustine knew as the Will of God, but now it can be manifest and real only through the death of God, or the transformation of an absolute transcendence into an absolute immanence.

Yet predestination remains itself in that very transformation, which is why I like to say that Augustine is the ancient name of

Nietzsche even as Nietzsche is the modern name of Augustine, for predestination is an absolute and eternal willing of Yes and No simultaneously; here the absolute Yes is absolutely unreal apart from the absolute No, so that nothing is a deeper illusion than an absolute Yes which is not an absolute No, or an absolute No which is not an absolute Yes. Is such an absolute No present in the Holocaust itself? Is this an absolute evil which is finally inseparable from an absolute good? Is the author of the Holocaust finally that Satan who is inseparable from Christ? Simply to raise the question of the Holocaust upon the horizon of an absolute Yes is to be open to such questions. Or is the Holocaust that one event which has annulled and dissolved every possible Yes? But would not an acceptance of such silence be a genuine victory of absolute evil?

Here, the Christian response to the Holocaust must be profoundly different than any possible response of the Jew, first, because the Christian is deeply responsible for the Holocaust, a responsibility which despite a certain Jewish orthodoxy is surely impossible for the Jew, and, second, the Christian unlike the Jew knows an ultimate redemption which is inseparable from an ultimate death, or an absolute good which is inseparable from an absolute evil. Just as it might be said that Satan is truly alien to the Jew, the Christian as Christian, or the Christian apart from a modern secularized Christianity, inevitably knows Satan, and knows Satan as the very opposite of Christ, and as that one who is conquered in the Crucifixion. Hence this opens up a uniquely Christian perspective upon the Holocaust, for if the Christian as Christian is the consequence of an ultimate and apocalyptic ending of Satan, or of the victory of eternal life over eternal death, then this very paradigm could be a way into the Holocaust itself, and into that Holocaust which is an absolute evil, or that Holocaust which is an epiphany of Satan. Jews often tell Christians that they can taste redemption, hence they know that they are living in an unredeemed world. Never has the Christian been more deeply open to this than in the Holocaust, if only here the Christian can know an absolute evil, and know it as being fully and actually real, and while many Christians say that it is the Holocaust which finally ended Christendom, it more deeply ended every God who can be known as Yes and only Yes, if it did not give us a God who can be known as No and only No.

But if Satan is truly the Lord of the Holocaust, then Satan is very much alive in our world, and even alive as God, or that God who is No and only No, or who is *mysterium tremendum* wholly apart from *mysterium fascinans*. This is the God whom Blake named as Satan, or the God whom our great American epic named as Moby-Dick (and Barth confessed that he primarily learned English so as to be able to read *Moby-Dick*). If it is the Holocaust which finally shattered every possible conception of evil, if was nevertheless a fulfillment of our deepest images of evil. Now an eternal darkness and abyss is truly incarnate, and if this is truly an incarnation, and perhaps the only incarnation which the Jew as Jew can know, then not only is it an absolute reversal of what the Christian knows as incarnation, but the Christian must become open to the possibility that this is a reversal only made possible by Christ, only made possible by that Word which became "flesh," or which has descended into the depths of Hell. Nothing is more revealing about Christianity than its ever increasing dissolution of the Descent into Hell, and this despite the overwhelming power of this motif in the Christian imagination; yet if the Christian must believe that Christ is present in the Holocaust, that could only be by way of a descent into Hell, that very Hell which Barth at the time of the Holocaust could declare is objectively impossible for all. Yet the Christian knows the descent into Hell as a final consequence of the Crucifixion itself; only in Hell does a final victory ultimately occur, and apart from that victory every other victory must finally be an illusion.

So it is that eternal death is just as essential for the Christian as is eternal life. This ultimate Christian truth is first theologically formulated by Paul, thence it was reborn in both Augustine and Luther, and even reborn in Nietzsche himself, our deepest atheist, and yet our deepest enactor of an absolute Yes. Is it possible that this Yes or any Yes could be said to the Holocaust? And, if not, can an absolute and eternal Yes ever be said again? Or is it the deepest mystery of the Holocaust that here an absolute No is finally an absolute Yes? If such a Yes cannot be pronounced, then finally our history is an absolute No, and even if it is history itself which comes to an end in the Holocaust, is that an ending which is finally a No and only a No, and hence a final epiphany of what the Christian knows as Satan? That would be a true and final reversal of crucifixion, and of incarnation itself, an apocalypse which is only a Satanic apocalypse, or an apocalypse of eternal darkness alone, and even if this is the apocalypse which is now most commonly called forth, is that the only apocalypse which now can be truly or actually named? Has Christianity not only finally ended, but in that very ending absolutely reversed itself? Or is this very ending finally a Christian reversal, and a Christian reversal of Christianity itself? These are ultimate questions which are inescapable for the Christian today, and it could be that the very ultimacy and mystery of our contemporary theological questions are a deep source of the apparent dissolution of theology today. If these are questions which we cannot meet, is an ultimate passivity our only destiny today?

CHAPTER 6

Art

In the winter of 1966, I received a call in my Emory office from a *Time* editor who was seeking assistance in the design for the cover of their Easter issue that year. They had intended for it to be a contemporary portrait of God but their research department had failed in its search for such a portrait, and he wondered if I could be of assistance. Fortuitously, and by a sheer coincidence, there happened to be in my office the one whom I regarded as the best authority on this subject, B. J. Stiles, and he was forced to tell the editor that he knew of no such portrait, and doubted if one could be possible. One result of this conversation is that the Easter issue of *Time* that year was designed in black, it did include yet another discussion of the death of God, and it proved to be the best-selling issue that *Time* has ever published. While I have never been able fully to enter contemporary painting, I have been deeply affected by modern painting, and I have come to believe that the late painting of both Van Gogh and Monet does center upon a uniquely modern portrait of God, and while God is unnamable as God in this painting, we nevertheless see God here, even if we thereby see a totality that is unnamable as God. Van Gogh has always been my favorite modern painter, and I believe that he has given us a unique icon of God, an absolutely alien God who is nevertheless a totally present God—a presence demanding a truly new seeing—and doing so by incorporating an icon dissolving every boundary between the sacred and the profane, and every boundary between center and circumference, or here and there.

While I have given a good deal of time to the study of art history and art criticism, as reflected in *History as Apocalypse*, which devotes its first chapter to Greek sculpture and a section of the Dante chapter to Giotto, I have only rarely discovered an actual theological study of art, and here I distinguish theological from iconographical analysis. There is an important distinction between an iconographical study, which is a historical analysis, and a theological study seeking to unveil an epiphany of the sacred in the work of art. The latter demands not only a religious sensibility but a religious empathy, and this is rare in scholars today. Art historians, of course, can find no assistance in the great body of our theology, which is indifferent to art; indeed, it is often if not commonly deeply hostile to art, and above all so in the modern world, where a truly sacred art has seemingly disappeared. However, there are paradoxes here, for just as a Calvinistic and iconoclastic Holland gave us our greatest modern portraiture, a seemingly religious America has given us virtually no religious painting at all, just as a profoundly secular modern France has given us a painting which is ever more fully becoming manifest as a truly new sacred painting, and perhaps most so in Cezanne. A deep *coincidentia oppositorum* of the sacred and the profane is manifest for all to see in a uniquely modern literature, but it is perhaps no less present in a uniquely modern art, and theology is now called upon to apprehend this *coincidentia*, which in large measure occurs in Mark Taylor's *Disfiguring*.

Our theology, however, inherits a tradition in which seeing is subordinate to hearing, and in our dominant modern theology authentic hearing is understood as effecting an iconoclastic negation of seeing, and if therein it deeply differs from the great body of ancient and medieval theology, this would appear to be a genuine reflection of a deeply modern condition. Is a uniquely modern condition one in which it is simply impossible to see the sacred, and is deep seeing for us inevitably and necessarily a purely profane seeing, or one in which the sacred can actually appear only as chaos or abyss? There can be little doubt that abyss and chaos are more fully manifest in our art than in any previous art, but can this be a genuine epiphany of the sacred for us? One in which a deep disfiguring or a deep dissolution is the inevitable vehicle of the sacred? Art historians and critics are open to the sacred as a category, but are reluctant to employ the word "God," and for good reason, for "God" has very nearly disappeared from our

critical discourse, and the very evocation of that word in critical circles is greeted with embarrassment or astonishment. So it is that twentieth-century philosophy differs most clearly from every previous
philosophy in the near absence of the very word "God," and so far
from being the queen of the sciences, theology today is little more
than their plaything or toy, and above all so any theology that dares to
employ the word "God."

William Hamilton published a collection of essays titled *On
Taking God Out of the Dictionary*, and this was a serious project.
Many if not most theologians were once taught to regard all dictionary
or common definitions of God as being the very opposite of a genuine
theological meaning of God, and this can clearly be seen in the very
usage of "God" in our common language, and if analytic philosophy is
devoted to decoding the meaning of our common language, it is clear
why it should have given us such shallow and empty meanings of
"God." And this is true not only of our common language but of our
dominant academic language, so that a theologian in our universities is
inevitably a missionary (or so I regarded myself), and a missionary not
to a "pagan" religious world, but to an "areligious" world, the first
such world in history, and this is commonly true even in scholarly
investigations of explicitly religious phenomena. I have come to
regard the American Academy of Religion as having become a deep
enemy not only of theology but of religion itself, for it is now far distant from the intention of its founders, and while this is perhaps an
inevitable evolution, it is revealing of our academic world, even if
there continues to remain a small body of scholars seeking genuine
religious and theological meaning.

To seek a theological meaning of art in such a world is certainly a
deep if not impossible challenge, and this challenge is compounded by
an arena dominated by formal and technical analysis, which is largely
true of art history today. This is something that I discovered at
Williams College, although their superb art department was the only
one there in which I found a home. Art history only entered the American university at a late date—another witness to an iconoclastic
America—yet it is also in America that art museums have truly
become sanctuaries, perhaps our only truly sacred sites; we treat art
museums as our cathedrals, and for a very good reason, for only here

can we discover today a truly holy ground. How could this be? What is there in art that evokes such a response, and does so in our seemingly most secular circles? The German theologian Moltmann once remarked that when God is dead religion is everywhere, and in some sense religion is everywhere today, but nowhere is such religion understood. Perhaps the world of art is that world which is most open to such an investigation; surely it is here that we moderns are most open to the sacred. But are we here most open to God? Ever since Barth's revolutionary commentary on the Epistle to the Romans, the theologian has been deeply suspicious of, if not hostile towards, religion, yet ironically this book is the most deeply religious of modern theological works, and most so in the very passages in which it assaults religion. That is dialectical theology, indeed, and such a dialectical theology does offer a way into the theological meaning of art, and one which concretely occurs here in Barth's analysis of Michelangelo's Sistine Chapel painting, where he perhaps most deeply draws forth the purely negative theological power of religion.

This is not simply a deeply modern Calvinism.Calvin would no doubt be horrified that Barth could take art so seriously, and this never occurs again in Barth's work, just as subsequent theological investigations of art, such as those of Tillich and his followers, never approach the power of the early Barth. But if dialectical theology can apprehend the purely negative power of art, if it is a genuinely dialectical theology, it can apprehend its positive or affirmative power, too; and this in the very context in which it knows its negative power, a negative power which dialectically must be a positive power, and one which we actually know in genuinely responding to art. There are those who believe that our modern museums of art are more truly holy than our classical museums, and it would appear to be undeniable that a traditional iconography is less powerful to us than is its modern parallel, with the exception of that art which is truly exotic to us, such as Byzantine art and Far Eastern painting, just as it also could be noted that the West only became open to such art in that fully modern world which has so comprehensively known the death of God.

Of course, the death of God is a primal icon of classical Christian painting and sculpture, or is so with the advent of Gothic art, and while the Crucifixion only very gradually entered Western art, and not truly so until after almost a thousand years of the evolution of that art, when this fully occurs it finally brings to an end every Western image of the Christ of Glory, or wholly overshadows every such image, so that in full modernity a true image of the resurrection has simply become impossible, or has become wholly inseparable from the image of Crucifixion. Thereby ancient Christian art is truly reversed, an art that could not or would not envision the Crucifixion, and this is just the point at which a classical Christian iconography passes into its fully modern equivalent, for iconography is truly universal, occurring as we now know in profoundly secular or "profane" expressions. This is not to say that we can yet understand such a profane iconography, nevertheless we must recognize it as iconography, and so recognize it if only because of its sacred status in our world. Modern painting has a sacred status for us going beyond any other art, and why has modern music never attained such a status? Certainly it is imaginatively as powerful as modern painting, and even if its very complexity would seem to confine it to an elite, its radical innovations are probably no greater than those of modern painting, and the sheer power of many of its expressions is undeniable. Is this because seeing for us is what hearing once was, or because we can now know a liberation in seeing that we cannot know in hearing, or cannot know in hearing without an enormous discipline and attention?

It is the mass popularity of modern art that is astounding, a popularity which is now virtually universal throughout the world. Here modern painting wholly transcends both modern music and modern poetry, and yet no one could think that its artists are greater artists, although perhaps its interpreters are far more effective priests or shamans, even having succeeded in making modern art or its counterfeit a primary vehicle of our advertising and mass media. Now it is simply not possible to counterfeit modern music or modern poetry, and if it is possible to counterfeit modern painting, and I often think that contemporary painting is little more than that, this is revealing of modern painting. So, too, art forgery abounds, and this is not only impossible in music and poetry, but simply inconceivable, so that one is reminded of the forgery of holy relics. This calls attention to the deep importance of touch in painting, one alien to both music and poetry, but truly integral in painting, even if for the great majority of viewers this can only be a vicarious touching. Yet we do touch painting in truly seeing it; painting is the only art in which this faculty is primary, and perhaps painting was always originally an icon. As we can see in the earliest painting known to us, we can see an icon only by touching it. Not only are sight and touch here inseparable, but sight is touch, and perhaps that is what it most deeply is in modern painting.

I know that I touch Van Gogh's paintings when I fully see them, and therein they truly are an icon to me; no classical or traditional Christian painting has such an effect upon me, and if only here I know that I, too, live in a sacred world. Perhaps it is sacred because it is only approachable through touch, that faculty seemingly least affected by modernity, unless in late modernity it has become so hollow as to be empty, and so empty as only to be awakened by an icon. Already Blake, on the first plate of *Europe*, could know our senses as now being so disordered that they are wholly isolated from one another, and only touch can find a passageway out of our fallen world. This was surely a fundamental reason why painting and design are so important in Blake's engravings of his prophetic poetry, and here for the first time in modernity a book is book and painting at once, which is one reason why art historians cannot understand Blake. Yet if finally we can only approach painting through touch, or through a seeing that is seeing and touch at once, then we can see why deep painting is inevitably a sacred painting, for it is inevitably an icon. The public response to modern art would seem to demonstrate that, and perhaps the deeply non-mimetic ground of modern art makes this possible; here we see as we cannot otherwise see, and yet we can know this seeing as pure seeing itself, and a pure seeing liberating us from our fallen or inverted senses.

Now it is true that there is an ultimate non-mimetic ground of modern music and poetry, but if only thereby they are deeply alien to the great body of humanity, whereas the non-mimetic ground of modern painting may well be a decisive key to its overwhelming and universal impact. It is precisely that world which we most openly and spontaneously see in full modernity that is most alien to us, most distant from any primordial or ancient vision, and certainly most distant from anything that we could recognize as a sacred vision. Yes, sight is our primary sensory faculty, and never more so than in modernity, when as Blake knew, our senses are most isolated from each other, so that now sight is naked and alone as it never was before, and hence if only because of its greater power more in need of liberation than our other senses. When the possibility of that liberation arises, as it does in modern painting, we overwhelmingly respond. But we could never so respond if we saw here what we see elsewhere, or what we have seen before; only a truly new seeing could liberate our sight, one which has never occurred before, yet when it does occur, as Proust knew so deeply in responding to Impressionism, it occurs as a renewal of a sight which we have lost, for the only true paradise is always the paradise we have lost. Such a response is simply not possible for modern music and poetry, or possible only for a few, whereas virtually everyone can respond to modern painting, or could do so once it had been established as a sacred art.

Our museums are sanctuaries as our concert halls and libraries are not, books may well be more widely distributed than paintings, but it is art books that are our sacred books, far more so than books of poetry are, and even when they are only coffee-table books, those are the very books that we are most eager to display; it is original paintings and not manuscripts which command astronomical prices in our marketplace, and this despite the fact that only a few experts allied with our most advanced scientific detection can distinguish an original painting from a forgery. I shall never forget the deep impact that William Gaddis's *The Recognitions* had upon me, our richest theological novel since *Moby-Dick*, for this is not only the novel that is our fullest portrait of New York, but it is a novel in which an art forger is a truly modern Christ figure, and whereas this is a truly demonic world, and a demonic and holy world at once, the forger is the only true innocent within it, and his innocence is inseparable from his forgery, a forgery giving life in a universal world of death, as here a forgery exactly faithful to the spirit and the letter of its Flemish masters re-creates the paintings of those masters so as to offer a strange kind of redemption. Thereby we are awakened to the power of a forgery which recalls the power of forged relics, yet all relics are forged, or all of our most sacred relics. Here there is no real distinction between the original and the copy, or the original and the "fake," for a true relic is wholly the product of the beholder, and its power resides precisely in that. Could that be true of modern art?

No, certainly not, and yet there is a power in all art deriving from its beholder. If we are awakened here as we are nowhere else, that very awakening is an ultimate power, and it occurs in modern art as it does nowhere else, or universally occurs here as it does nowhere else, and that may well be true in every historical world. There are no "atheists" in the presence of genuine art, or none who are unawakened to the sacred. Here is a real presence, indeed, and it can occur even in the midst of the deepest spiritual darkness. Perhaps only that darkness makes possible the power of modern art, just as only a seeing that is wholly other than our common seeing makes possible the seeing of modern painting, and just as there is a universal ritual throughout the world, a truly cosmic mass, there is a universal art throughout the world. Each conveys the sacred to our most immediate actuality, and each only does so by isolating itself from its own world, or its apparent world, or what Hegel knew as "the given." The truth is that religion has never occurred apart from art, and even Buddhism, the most iconoclastic of all religions, evolved the most comprehensive of all iconographies, just as Islam evolved a truly iconoclastic art, which is also true of Judaism, and even true of the purest Calvinism, and if modern art is finally a truly sacred art, it is also our most deeply iconoclastic art, and one whose dissolution or disfiguring of every given sacred image nevertheless evolved a truly sacred image in that very disfiguring or dissolution, and a sacred image which for the first time is open to all and everyone.

Is the theologian called upon to discover God in modern art? A seemingly impossible calling, yet our truly modern poetry is unthinkable apart from a profound wrestling with or defiance of God, and all of our great modern composers have been deeply religious, perhaps the most deeply religious body of artists who ever lived. So, too, there has never been a more religious painter than Van Gogh, or a more holy one, and it is Van Gogh who is the most popular of modern painters, and if ever there was a God-obsessed painter, this is Van Gogh, and above all the final Van Gogh of breakdown, insanity, and suicide. I believe that *Wheatfield with Crows* is our purest modern image of God. This is the painting that I would now choose to be on that *Time* cover, and if this is an image of crucifixion, it is simultaneously an image of resurrection; here resurrection is crucifixion, and it is most deeply so in the very absence of all traditional iconography. This makes possible its ultimate immediacy, and its ultimate immediacy for us, an immediacy comprehending the whole horizon of this painting. The pure absence of every traditional icon or image makes possible here a truly new icon, one which we can actually touch, but only touch in a touching that consumes us, and if this is a touch that is a way out of our fallen world, it is just thereby a way into its deepest depths, as here we are given a paradise that is certainly lost, and precisely thereby a paradise for us.

But how could this possibly be an image of God? It will not do simply to say with Tillich that this is so because it evokes an ultimate response. This fails to say anything at all about the imagery that here is so dazzlingly present, an imagery seemingly evoking the total absence or emptiness of God; and yet its very darkness, and its overwhelming darkness, evokes the total presence of God, a total presence in that very darkness, and a total presence as that very darkness. Thereby that darkness is a joyous darkness, and we can only say Yes in response to it, even if that is saying Yes to the deepest and most ultimate No. Here, the No is said only for the sake of the Yes, and if here we can only see an absolute No, that very seeing is a joyous Yes, and a joyous Yes impossible apart from the depths of this vision of darkness, or apart from the depths of this absolute No. And we can know this Yes only because we can taste this No. Now we absorb a darkness which is totality itself, a darkness here which is a dazzling light, but that light is the light of darkness itself, not only a light impossible apart from darkness, but a light indistinguishable from darkness, and if thereby we consume the dead or dying God, that consumption is resurrection itself, a resurrection which is Yes and only Yes. Is there no theology that can enter this painting, or finally no theology that can enter any great painting, or can be open to a final and ecstatic Yes?

Byzantine theology seemingly could, but that theology is vastly distant from us, and a contemporary Byzantine theology is simply unknown; moreover, not even Catholic theology can truly enter Giotto's painting, and yet Giotto gave us an imagery in which there is a true and actual union of the humanity and the divinity of Christ, one which Christian theology could affirm as its deepest dogma but could never conceptually or systematically draw forth. If this is the deepest mystery of Christianity, it is profoundly unveiled by Giotto, and unveiled even in our world by Van Gogh, and, yes, unveiled in *Wheatfield with Crows*, for here the very coalescence of crucifixion and resurrection is a coalescence of the humanity and the divinity of Christ. Van Gogh's own overt images of Christ simply collapse in the horizon of this painting, but so, too, does every traditional image of Christ, and every traditional image of God; and if modern art is the first Western art to dissolve all images of God, this is a dissolution making possible an ultimate rebirth, and even a rebirth of images of God, which I believe deeply occurs in the late painting of both Van Gogh and Monet, and perhaps of Cezanne, too, if we only had the theological mind to comprehend it. Yes, here we can know the death of God as the resurrection of God, but not the resurrection of the Lord of Glory, not a resurrection which is an ascension into Heaven, but rather a resurrection which is a descent into Hell, a resurrection which is an ecstatic Yes to the depths of darkness, one wherein the deepest darkness is not transfigured into the deepest light, but wherein that darkness *is* the deepest light.

I have long been enchanted by Monet's water lilies, and fascinated, too, a fascination that I associate with Rudolf Otto's *mysterium fascinans*, the positive or affirmative pole of the holy, and while for Otto this never truly occurs apart from the *mysterium tremendum*, I think that in these water lilies we are given a *mysterium fascinans* wholly apart from a *mysterium tremendum*. This is just why we cannot say "God" in response to this vision of paradise, nor even remember the God whom we have known, but if we are here truly given a moment of grace, we cannot finally dissociate it from "God." Hence the very disappearance of God, or the pure invisibility of God, could make possible a total presence of God. Deep mystics have long known this, but that mysticism at least in the West has been profoundly aniconic, and if these water lilies are truly an image of God, that visibility is only made possible by a pure invisibility, an invisibility in which we lose every God whom we have been given, but precisely thereby we "see" God, and see God in these water lilies. And this is a vision of God not only made possible by the invisibility of God, but the paintings themselves enact that invisibility; their very calling forth of the pure immediacy of this pond and these lilies is an enactment of that invisibility. We can only see this water and these flowers by seeing them as totality itself; here we actually see that totality, but we do so only when every trace of God has vanished, and we can only see these paintings by actually seeing the pure emptiness of God, for only that emptiness makes possible a seeing of the invisibility of God.

Unlike Van Gogh, there is not a trace of any iconography in Monet. Monet along with Cezanne is our most purely profane modern painter. Nor is there even an echo of a *mysterium tremendum*. Now every *mysterium tremendum* is absolutely silent and invisible, and only that invisibility and silence makes possible such a pure *mysterium fascinans*, a *mysterium fascinans* which here undergoes an epiphany as totality itself. If only for this reason this epiphany is alien to everything that we can name as God, yet it is clearly an epiphany, one simply undeniable to its viewer, and the theologian must identify it as an epiphany of the sacred, and perhaps most so because it is not an epiphany of God. Is this a genuine *coincidentia oppositorum* of the sacred and the profane, and one in which both the sacred as sacred and the profane as profane are dissolved, or in which each fully passes into the other, and in which we are given a seeing in which we can see the sacred only by seeing the profane and can see the profane only by seeing the sacred? Thereby we actually see a pure moment of incarnation, and a moment which here and now is all in all, so that now Earth itself is actually paradise, and paradise in this absolutely joyous moment.

The Christian knows the death of God or the Crucifixion as the one source of redemption, but theologically we have never known a total death of God, or not known it in a purely theological language. Yet such a redemption seemingly appears in these water lilies, and we can see this redemption only by losing every vision of God. Is this a movement in some sense occurring in every genuine expression of modern art, and could this be a fulfillment of an authentic Christian tradition, one wholly obscured or reversed by our theologies, but nevertheless deeply present in our fullest and purest painting? We could call upon the Christian epic tradition as a way into what may well be an epic tradition of painting, and if there is a genuine continuity between Dante and Joyce, there may well be a genuine continuity between Giotto and Cezanne. Giotto was our first epic painter, the first artist to give us a truly epic enactment of the life of Christ. Is that an enactment which is repeated in our deepest modern painting, and repeated in a Kierkegaardian repetition which is a forward rather than a backward movement to eternity? Now eternity is the very opposite of any possible primordial eternity or totality, and only thereby is it absolutely and totally present.

It is my conviction that each of us is truly theological in deeply responding to art. This is surely one crucial point at which theology is a universal horizon, and even is so in our world; while we as yet have no real theological understanding of this ground, and cannot do so insofar as we are not open to a truly new theology, the necessity for a truly and even absolutely new theology is now clearly manifest. But is an absolutely new theology possible for us? Christian theologians often if not commonly believe that an absolutely new theology is embodied in the purest writing of Paul, which is one reason why it is so frequently believed that Paul created Christianity, but a comparable revolutionary theology is embodied in Augustine's purest writing, and if it was Augustine who created our uniquely Western theology, this very theology has undergone deep transformations in its history, and perhaps most so in the modern world. So a truly new theology would be in genuine continuity with this tradition, and while truly alien to the ecclesiastical theologian, it is manifest for all to see in the radical theological thinking of Hegel and Kierkegaard, and that is the very theological thinking which has had the deepest impact upon our world. Unless it is Nietzsche's theological thinking which has had that impact, and it is important to note that it is artists who first became open to Nietzsche's revolutionary thinking, and most clearly so in their enactments of the death of God. No other symbol has been more comprehensively powerful in twentieth-century painting and poetry, and perhaps nothing so fully turns us away from that poetry and painting than does a refusal of the death of God.

CHAPTER 7

Yes and No

When I was seventeen I was given the extraordinary good fortune of being able to interview Louis Armstrong, one whom I believe embodies pure genius itself, and while at this time during the Second World War he was undergoing, as he declared, tough breaks, he was already an icon in America. I had long been a jazz fan, although at that time I could only assemble a jazz record collection by visiting black homes, combing through their stored and dusty record collections, and buying what I could. I had absorbed the dominant judgment that *West End Blues* is Louis's greatest recording, and when our conversation ended, he asked if I had a request. Of course, I asked for "The West End Blues." "What's that?" he asked in perplexity. "Ain't never heard of it. Hum me a little to see if I know it." So I falteringly hummed, and he cried, "Oh, that!" and as his bandsmen reassembled after the intermission, he called for it without a title that I could recognize. Then I heard "The West End Blues" as I have never heard it before or since, and heard it with an ecstatic Yes. Perhaps nowhere else can we know such an immediate Yes than in listening to genuine jazz, one that is irresistible to its hearer, and one that I must inevitably know as a theological call, as a call to understand the theological ground of this Yes. So it is that when I was blocked in attempting to complete *Total Presence*, I immersed myself in jazz as I sought a way to an affirmation of that abyss and emptiness that is here called forth, thereby making possible the final paragraph of the book, which is all that I have ever published on jazz.

The arts have commonly had an ultimate impact upon me as I attempt to think theologically. Here I have found genuine inspiration, one open to all. In this perspective, too, theology can be understood as a universal horizon, for there is a depth in art that demands a theological response, or so I have long believed, and it is of prime importance that it is so extraordinarily difficult truly to distinguish the purest expressions of art and religion. It is also of fundamental importance that both the aesthetic and the religious consciousness or sensibility are truly universal; nor can firm lines be apprehended between them in our cultures and societies. It is as though art and religion are not truly or finally distinct, or not so in their deepest and purest expressions. Now if it is modernity alone which has created a truly profane or truly secular art, we can discover here as we can nowhere else in modernity an open expression of a *coincidentia oppositorum* of the sacred and profane, for our truly profane art is a truly sacred art, and is so most clearly in its very impact. It is the open and final Yes of that art which poses an ultimate theological problem or mystery, and if this is a Yes which is possible only in the depths of an ultimate No or an ultimate abyss, that very No is here finally a Yes, and is so even if we cannot comprehend it. But that it is said and enacted we cannot doubt, or cannot doubt apart from apathy and withdrawal, and even if apathy is universal in our new world, that very universality is a consequence of a deep history, and a history embodied in our imaginative history, and embodied here with a clarity and decisiveness manifest nowhere else.

Perhaps a comparable history is present in the history of our ethical thinking and sensibility, but this has not yet been called forth, except in Nietzsche's profound reversal of historical thinking, which unthinks Western ethical thinking itself. Such an unthinking of ethical thinking can be understood as a truly new and revolutionary ethical thinking, one that already occurs in Spinoza, and it does parallel the revolution effected by those ancient prophets who disenacted and reversed the ethical consciousness of their world, hence making possible Nietzsche's understanding of the slave revolt in morality. While this gave us the uniquely modern idea of *ressentiment*, nothing comparable to *ressentiment* is possible in an understanding of our imaginative history, for it is impossible for us to understand any genuine art as an expression of No-saying and No-saying alone. Already Nietzsche's initial understanding of Greek tragedy made possible for him an understanding of an ultimate No which is finally an ultimate Yes. This finally released the primal motif of his mature thinking, one at the very center of his final conflict with our nihilism, a conflict truly shattering Nietzsche himself. If Nietzsche could call forth an absolute Yessaying that is finally an absolute Yes-saying to absolute No-saying itself, this does open up the mystery of our uniquely modern imaginative nihilism, a nihilism finally reversing itself, and reversing itself even in its most purely negative expressions.

This has been a major, if not the major, motif in our deeper hermeneutical unveiling of the modern imagination, one that has profoundly affected me, and without which I could not be a theologian. But is it possible not to think theologically in understanding an absolute No as finally being an absolute Yes? Can we understand tragedy itself without thinking theologically, or fully understand our deeper modern painting and poetry without understanding them theologically? These are certainly impossibilities for me, but my thinking has only all too gradually entered such realms, being fundamentally blocked by all of our existing or manifest theological thinking, and to the extent that liberation has occurred for me, it has only occurred through what the theological world can only recognize as an anti-theological thinking. Yet it is possible to understand a profoundly anti-theological thinking and vision as being overwhelmingly powerful in a uniquely modern imagination, certainly a vision and thinking effecting a dissolution or reversal of all of our given or manifest theological understanding, but thereby it is in genuine continuity with our deeper imaginative history. Already in Homer and in Greek tragedy we can observe such a reversal, a reversal also occurring in the Christian epic tradition from Dante through Joyce, and if it is the purest expressions of the imagination which are the deepest challenges to faith, these nevertheless demand a theological exploration, and do so in their very imagery and language.

I have long known Kafka as the purest challenge to theology in the twentieth century. None of our theologians are so purely theological as is Kafka, a theological purity inseparable from Kafka's writing itself. Here we have been given purely theological inscriptions, and inscriptions truly reversing every possible theological understanding. While Kafka seldom writes the word "God," nothing is more absent from Kafka's writing than the absence of God. Nowhere else in our world may one discover such a pure guilt, or such a pure abyss; and while a uniquely modern abyss and guilt, these are inseparable from the total presence of an absolute and final *mysterium tremendum*, one which is an absolute judgment and an absolute judgment alone. It was Walter Strauss who was my primary guide into Kafka's writing, and while he can read it as an inverted or reverse Kabbalah which is impossible for me, I cannot deny that this is a way whereby the way up is the way down, just as I cannot deny that the very purity of Kafka's No is finally an ultimate Yes. Buber was the only theologian who deeply responded to Kafka while Kafka was writing, and in his discussion of Kafka in *Two Types of Faith*, he can conclude by affirming that the eclipse of God which here occurs does not diminish the immediacy of God. In that very immediacy God remains "the Savior," and the contradiction of existence becomes for us a theophany. These are extraordinarily daring words theologically, and they disappear in Buber's later understanding of the eclipse of God, but they do unveil an absolute No as an absolute Yes, and if this is possible even in Kafka's writing, that impossible possibility offers us the genuine possibility of a truly new theological understanding.

Theologians such as Reinhold Niebuhr once accused me of being closed to all possible mystery, but I think that the very reverse of this is true. I am far rather imprisoned by mystery rather than liberated from it, and although I have adopted Hegel as my philosophical master, I have done so only by conjoining Hegel and Nietzsche, thereby refusing Hegel's pure dissolution of mystery, and his consequent dissolution of theology itself, even if theology is here truly reborn into a pure and total philosophy. A Hegelian Yes is a purely conceptual or purely logical Yes, one wholly transcending every possible interior expression, and while the *Science of Logic* can offer a purely logical argument for that "cunning of reason" which is teleology or theodicy (in the second section of its second volume), and conclude by declaring God to be "pure personality," this is nonetheless a purely logical thinking in which all interiority is finally impossible, as Kierkegaard knew so deeply. Nevertheless, Hegel's philosophy is our fullest philosophy of art, and our fullest philosophy of religion as well, and just as Hegel is the only philosopher who has given us comprehensive understandings of both art and religion, his is our only full and perhaps our only actual philosophy of history.

Karl Loewith, one of the few who has mastered both Hegel and Nietzsche, had a real impact upon me in arguing that faith can only know the deep meaninglessness of history, whereas it is only purely secular expressions of thinking that can know the meaning and order of history (I heard this argument in his classroom before it was published in *Meaning in History*). Loewith is here under the impact of both Kierkegaard and Barth, and while he was my only theological ally as a graduate student, I was forced to depart from this way in my own theological thinking, and the primal reason for this is what I ever more comprehensively came to apprehend as the ultimate theological necessity of a total Yes. This is a Yes that Hegel comprehensively understands and enacts, but a Yes that can never be separated or isolated from an absolute No, and Hegel deeply understands an absolute No in his very understanding of self-negation or self-emptying. Yet this is a No which not Hegel but Nietzsche profoundly understands interiorly, which is just why Nietzsche is absolutely necessary to Hegel, and only thereby can a purely and totally dialectical thinking actually be meaningful and real to us. Hence full dialectical thinking is inseparable from a pure and total *coincidentia oppositorum*, a true and actual *coincidentia oppositorum* of an absolute Yes and an absolute No, and if this occurs in all genuine dialectical thinking, as perhaps most purely embodied in Mahayana Buddhist philosophy, it also can be understood as occurring in our deepest imaginative enactments, and perhaps most clearly so in a uniquely modern imagination.

This is the very imagination that our dominant theological thinking ultimately opposes, yet the primary texts of this imagination can be understood as sacred texts or scripture. Here we have been given a truly canonical writing, a writing demanding not only pure attention but pure absorption. Such attention has certainly occurred in our world, but could it occur apart from what the theologian names as revelation? Of course, this could be a false, or illusory, or demonic revelation, and it surely has induced what the theologian can name as idolatry; but idolatry is a truly elusive theological category, and if the deepest idolatry inevitably evokes the deepest iconoclasm, this first occurs in the prophetic revolution of Israel; but this is an iconoclasm most fundamentally directed against the worship of Yahweh, or the worship of Yahweh in its world, and every subsequent expression of this iconoclasm has been an assault upon the dominant theological naming of its own world. Thereby we can understand the modern imagination itself as being profoundly iconoclastic, and if we can discover a genuine rebirth of the ancient prophets in a Van Gogh or a Kafka, this is the rebirth of an absolute judgment, and an absolute judgment enacted and pronounced in that language and imagery most immediately real to us. Is it idolatrous to look upon the painting of Van Gogh or the writing of Kafka as scripture for us, or is it far rather idolatrous to refuse this scripture as genuine scripture, and refuse it if only because it is not an ecclesiastically sanctioned scripture?

These questions were driving questions for me, and they revolve about the possibility of a truly secular theology, or a truly incarnate or embodied theology, a theology open to the theological power of its own world, and of that world which we actually confront. Yet if we can see that fundamentalism is a false or illusory way, and also see that a post-Barthian neo-orthodoxy is equally unreal, and unreal if only because of its deep alienation from our world, then both Augustine and Kierkegaard could once again become real theological models for us. Each profoundly embodied his own historical world, even if they deeply transfigured those worlds. Just as Augustine discovered the very subject of consciousness, so also Kierkegaard discovered a uniquely modern subjectivity, and while this is a subjectivity only implicitly known by a Descartes, it is truly real with the birth of full modernity, a modernity calling forth an interiority that is wholly inseparable from its purely negative ground. Of course, this is true of Augustine, too, who could discover a freedom of the will that is inseparable from the impotence of the will, and just as both Augustine and Kierkegaard are truly dialectical in their understanding of freedom and grace, this could be renewed in an even more comprehensive form in our world, but only as a consequence of a voyage into that interiority which is most actual and real for us. This is just the point at which every neo-orthodox theology collapses, for it cannot actually enter its own world, and therefore it is inevitably an alien theology, and most alien to its own world.

I have most defied my theological masters and peers by choosing Nietzsche as a theological master, and even if I understand Nietzsche as the culmination of a long theological tradition, he certainly reverses that and every theological tradition, and can justly be understood as the greatest anti-theological thinker in history. How is it possible for a theologian to become a Nietzschean and to remain a theologian? First, it is possible because it is true of Nietzsche himself.

Now just as Nietzsche could unveil every Western philosopher as being at bottom a theologian, no one else has had such a comprehensive understanding of theology; and it cannot be denied that Nietzsche's work is pervaded by an explicitly theological language, and far more so than that of any other modern philosopher apart from Spinoza and Hegel, and even Nietzsche's most ecstatic language is often a clearly theological language, occurring not only in his proclamation of the death of God, but also occurring in his most deeply negative hermeneutics, as in his very discovery of genealogy itself. Here, genealogy ultimately derives from the very advent of the "bad conscience," a bad conscience which is a purely negative or purely repressed consciousness, one which Nietzsche understands as the advent of an absolute No-saying, and an absolute No-saying which has only actually or only historically been named in the naming of the uniquely Christian God.

While the slave revolt in morality, or the advent of *ressentiment* itself, occurred in the prophetic revolution of Israel, it is only consummated in the birth of Christianity, which Nietzsche came to know as the only ultimate catastrophe which has occurred in history, so that he could know the death of the Christian God as the only possible source of liberation for humanity, and Nietzsche is our only modern philosopher of an absolute liberation or an absolute redemption, although here he does unveil his deeply Hegelian ground. Not even Kierkegaard could actually think redemption, and while Augustine does truly think redemption, at no other point is he so clearly or perhaps so deeply a Neoplatonic or pagan thinker, and most decisively so because he understands redemption as eternal return; and all too significantly the scholastic theological understanding of redemption is an understanding of eternal return, that very eternal return or "recollection" which Kierkegaard himself could understand as being deeply and purely pagan. Indeed, Nietzsche is that very thinker who has most profoundly reversed every possible understanding of eternal return, and done so in his very discovery of an absolutely new eternal recurrence, an eternal recurrence reversing every movement of eternal return, and doing so most decisively in its final shattering of every possible transcendence, which itself is only possible as a consequence of the death of God. Only Nietzsche has actually thought an apocalyptic redemption, for while this occurs in Hegel, here it occurs in a wholly abstract mode, whereas for Nietzsche the thinking of an apocalyptic redemption is the very enactment of an absolute Yes and Amen.

Clearly this is a truly theological thinking, and while theologians have understood it as a profoundly anti-theological thinking, it can be understood as a deep reversal and inversion of a theological thinking and tradition which Kierkegaard could already understand both as a betrayal of faith and as culminating in the end of Christendom. It is difficult to doubt that Kierkegaard and Nietzsche are true twins—polar twins it is true, even opposite twins—but not only are they humanly very much alike, but also alike as linguistic and poetic creators, and truly parallel to each other in their unique understandings of the depths of subjectivity or interiority itself, and of the absolutely primary role of God in those depths. Nietzsche understands the very birth of interiority as the consequence of the advent of an absolute No-saying or "God," thereby fully paralleling a Kierkegaardian understanding of *Angst* or dread or the sickness unto death, an *Angst* only possible as the consequence of an absolute negation or refusal of God; and the understanding of interiority or subjectivity for both Kierkegaard and Nietzsche becomes ever more fully theological as it evolves, so that it is only a younger Kierkegaard and a younger Nietzsche who can fully write about the aesthetic, just as the mature Kierkegaard and the mature Nietzsche cannot write without breaking the boundaries of writing itself. Each thinker was a profoundly solitary thinker, perhaps the most solitary creative thinkers who have ever lived, and just as each has given us our most profound solitary thinking, each of them was finally alone, and to this day they remain alone as theological thinkers.

These are only a few of the reasons why I was so deeply attracted to Nietzsche, indeed, hypnotized by Nietzsche, and this was true of many of my theological friends and allies as well. Nietzsche's pure theological genius is undeniable; the real question revolves about the problem of whether or not Nietzsche is truly and finally a purely pathological theological thinker. Not even Tillich could bring himself to reach this judgment, and just as Tillich was inspired by Nietzsche, and so much so that many critics doubt that there is anything that finally separates them theologically, I began to believe that this is true of Bultmann, too, and certainly of that radical Bultmannianism into which I had been initiated. So at this point I am sympathetic with the assault of orthodox theologians upon both Tillich and Bultmann, but both Kierkegaard and Nietzsche ended theological liberalism even more deeply than they ended theological orthodoxy, and true conservatives have been drawn to both Nietzsche and Kierkegaard because of their profound subversion of all modern liberalism.

One of the principles that I absorbed as a theological student is that genuine faith cannot only absorb the deepest possible challenge but that it becomes even more truly faith in meeting such a challenge. Once again Augustine is a true model here, but so, too, are Pascal and Kierkegaard and Dostoyevsky. Is such a movement of faith impossible in late modernity? A dialectical principle is fully present here, that the deepest or truest faith is not possible apart from the deepest No to that faith, and this principle is fully present in all genuine apocalypticism, for an apocalyptic light can only be manifest and real in the purest darkness, just as that light itself can only dawn in a horizon of total darkness. Already this is true in the prophetic revolution of Israel, which is one reason why that revolution is the genuine seed or source of apocalypticism, and just as Christian theology has ever more fully distanced itself from apocalypticism, despite its origin in the purely apocalyptic theology of Paul, it has thereby not only lost or transformed its original biblical ground, but ever more fully dissolved dialectical thinking itself. True, this has been reborn in Christian revolutionaries such as Augustine, Luther, and Kierkegaard, but reborn even more comprehensively in Hegel and Nietzsche, and if it is Hegel and Nietzsche who are our deepest modern apocalyptic thinkers, they call forth an absolute apocalypse that is an absolute reversal of everything once manifest and real as the uniquely Christian God.

Nietzsche, above all other thinkers, could know the very birth of Christianity as an absolute reversal of Jesus, and while this only occurs in *The Antichrist*, his last full or complete writing, it occurs as the first volume of what was intended to be his magnum opus, "The Revaluation of All Values." Only in the closing months of his creativity could Nietzsche know that in Christianity the gospel or "good news" of Jesus becomes *dysangel*, and everything that Jesus proclaimed and enacted becomes the very opposite of itself. There is a theology much like this in the dialectical thinking of the early Barth, but this is almost wholly lost in *Church Dogmatics*, except for its most radical sections, and just as Barth deeply turned away from

Kierkegaard in becoming a dogmatician, he thereby turned away from dialectical thinking itself, and since that time genuine dialectical theological thinking has seemingly disappeared. In choosing to become a dialectical theologian I thought of myself as remaining loyal to the early Barth, for it was Barth and not Tillich who was my modern theological model, and while this demands a genuine betrayal of Barth, I joined many other theologians in thinking that it was Barth himself who had most deeply betrayed Barth. This is not unheard of in the history of theology—one has only to think of the late Luther— nor is it unheard of in the history of philosophy, as witness both Plato and Hegel, but it is unheard of in our imaginative history, unheard of in our greatest artists and poets. It is as though the genuine artist has been given a vocation that cannot be betrayed, and if only here there is an ultimate distinction between thinking and the imagination.

Of course, both Kierkegaard and Nietzsche crossed every division between thinking and the imagination, and while the thinking of each deeply transformed itself in the course of its development, it nonetheless remains truly consistent with itself in that very development, and although Kierkegaard's thinking seemingly culminates with a total and final No, Nietzsche's culminates with a final and total Yes, and this despite the fact that madness finally consumed him. Is that very madness a decisive sign of the pathological ground of this Yes, and was it thereby an inevitable consequence of that unique way which Nietzsche had enacted, and thus a paradigmatic model of the consequences of every true rebellion against God? Many theologians view Nietzsche's madness in this way, just as many assert that there is no possible genuine atheism, or none which is not pathological and deranged. And this leads to a fundamental question: Is atheism an actual possibility, and has it ever truly and actually occurred? I became much taken with Lucien Fabre's book on Rabelais, which argues that atheism did not come into existence historically until the end of the sixteenth century, but it soon gains an ultimate historical power, and it played a decisive role in the French Revolution, that most paradigmatic of all modern historical events, so that both Blake and Hegel could know the French Revolution as the dawning of a universal death of God. Certainly atheism is not an illusion in this context, unless modernity itself is finally an illusion, an illusion now coming to an end, so that conservative theologians can greet "postmodernity" as a liberation from an illusory or pathological modernity.

Nevertheless, the question of the possibility of a real atheism is both a genuine and an inescapable theological question, and if it is only in the modern world that we can speak of a deep atheism, that is an atheism that can be and has been discovered in all of our genuinely modern philosophical thinking, and one that has ever more comprehensively pervaded a uniquely modern society and world. Indeed, there are those who understand atheism as an inevitable expression of faith itself. This has become my own position, but I did not reach it apart from a genuine struggle, and with many false paths; here I can see no organic development in my own thinking, and if my theological voyage has been one into an ever deeper atheism, it has nonetheless become ever fuller theologically in that very atheism. Of course, there is a kind of atheism in deep mysticism, one finally dissolving every image and idea of God, but it is clear that such a movement realizes a God or Godhead beyond "God," or beyond everything that is given us or is manifest as God. So, too, there is a penultimate atheism which can be understood as essential to faith, one dissolving or negating every God who is manifest apart from the depths of faith, which is to say every God whom we commonly know and name. But these are not final atheisms, and the real question here is whether or not a final or ultimate atheism is possible.

Most theologians affirm that the apparent atheism of our world is an illusory atheism, one which is deeply groundless, and will inevitably wither away when depth is called forth. But this is an extraordinarily difficult task theologically, and above all so in our world, so that Barth was wise in condemning all such apologetics, which he could know as a betrayal of faith, and surely our apologetics has been incapable of employing a language of depth which atheists can recognize as their own. I believe that it is theologically irresponsible to think that atheism is an illusion. Here I side with the fundamentalists who know modernity as a deep and ultimate atheism, and, so, too, inevitably side at this point with those conservative theologians who know modernity itself as an absolute negation of God. I simply do not see how this can genuinely be denied, and it is certainly a fundamental reason why our liberal theologies have withered away. I also believe that there is an ultimate Either-Or here, which I attempted to formulate in the concluding chapter of *The Gospel of Christian Atheism*: either a traditional faith or a uniquely modern atheism, for I can find no middle way between them. Here, I alienated myself from my theological friends, but I did not and do not see how I could have avoided this, even if I could have prosecuted it far more adroitly. Yet it is absolutely crucial here to understand our uniquely modern atheism, and while I do not think that I was irresponsible in choosing Blake, Hegel, and Nietzsche as being deep and pure embodiments of this atheism, this does bring our atheism into a new perspective, for this is a genuinely theological atheism, and one which I was persuaded can be understood as a Christian atheism. Then atheism itself is given a new theological meaning, for deep atheism is not simply a negation, it is an ultimate affirmation in that very negation, and that affirmation occurs in its very negation of God, and above all in its deep and ultimate negation of the uniquely Christian God.

This is most clear in Nietzsche, but it is most comprehensive in Hegel, and most visionary in Blake, and all of these negations are truly missing in modern theology, which impels one to ask if we have yet been given a truly modern theology, or a theology which can be truly or fully meaningful in our world. Moreover, Blake, Hegel, and Nietzsche speak more fully or more comprehensively of God than any other modern writers. One could even say that their very language is inseparable from our deepest modern language about God. Is this a language that simply cannot be entered theologically, or only entered with a language of assault and refusal? The theologian also has grave difficulty in responding to an ultimate heresy, but the question can be asked if there is a single modern artist or thinker who is not a deep heretic, and heretical not only interiorly, but heretical in their deepest enactments. A dramatic demonstration of this occurs in Cornelius Fabro's *God in Exile*, a stunning and comprehensive history of modern philosophical atheism, surely the best study of its kind, and one wherein we can understand our atheism as becoming ever deeper and more comprehensive in its very organic development or evolution. Such philosophical atheism is the very opposite of a simple or literal atheism, for it occurs in the purity of thinking itself; nor can agnosticism be found in this atheism, an agnosticism alien to genuine thinking. No, our philosophical atheism is a truly heretical atheism, and it is genuinely heretical in its very negation of the Christian God. If Nietzsche is our last metaphysical thinker, as Heidegger affirms, he is our purest metaphysical atheist, yet here is a metaphysical atheism which is a truly theological atheism, one only possible by way of the deepest and most ultimate negation of God.

Most theologians think that such a negation is purely illusory, but it is very difficult to deny that this has actually occurred in the modern world, and, most baffling to the theologian, occurred most deeply by way of the very language and movement of faith itself. This is clearest in Blake and Hegel, and just as Blake is our most biblical modern poet, Hegel is our only philosopher who has employed the purest language of faith in his deepest philosophical realizations. In Hegel and in Hegel alone the ultimate movements of creation, fall, incarnation, crucifixion, and resurrection are realized in a purely philosophical thinking, and, most paradoxically of all, this occurs by way of a philosophical realization of the death of God, which occurs for the first time in the *Phenomenology of Spirit*, and if this is our most revolutionary modern philosophical work, it is inseparable from the passage of the Crucifixion itself into the depths of thinking. But at this very time, Blake's revolutionary imaginative vision was incorporating these primal theological movements, embodying for the first time a truly radical vision into the fullness of the imagination, one inseparable from a comprehensive enactment of the death of God, and for the first time the death of God is fully enacted imaginatively. To this day, our theologians refuse to recognize these revolutionary breakthroughs as Christian enactments, and this despite the fact that an explicitly Christian language is more primal for Blake and Hegel than it is for any other modern poet or thinker. Are they refused by our theologians because they are such ultimate heretics, surely the deepest heretics in our history? It is remarkable how little attention is given in modern theology to all deep and ultimate heresy, and this despite its overwhelming power in our world. It is as though such heresy is theologically unspeakable, and this is doubly ironic for the Christian theologian, since both Jesus and Paul are portrayed as heretics in the New Testament.

I often wonder if I am a deeper heretic than my more distinguished peers, and even wondered if it is possible to be a genuine theologian without being a heretic. Can one forget that Aquinas himself was once assaulted by high ecclesiastical authority as a heretic? Newman created modern historical theology by identifying the ancient heresies as dead fossils marking false and lifeless paths in the organic evolution of Christian doctrine, and while our modern heresies may be false, they are certainly very much alive, and surely more alive in our world than are our modern theological orthodoxies. Both Hegel and Blake assaulted the theological orthodoxies of their world as being truly non-Christian, and Hegel could understand such orthodoxy in a way fully paralleling Newman's understanding of heresy; for it is orthodoxy itself which ceases to evolve in the modern world, which alone is a decisive sign of its non-Christian ground. Newman was impelled into his evolutionary theological thinking by a realization of the immense distance between modern Catholic dogma and the New Testament, but now what is seemingly only a Catholic theological problem has been realized as a universal Christian theological problem, and nowhere has it been more deeply resolved than in Hegel's evolutionary understanding of the profound transformation of the Western world as a whole, one certainly comprehending a transformation of Christian dogma, and the deepest possible transformation of that dogma. Inevitably, this is an ultimate transformation of the deepest Christian dogma, one surely occurring in both Blake and Hegel, but that transformation is in genuine continuity with a uniquely Christian history, for Christianity alone among the great religions of the world has profoundly transformed itself in its very historical embodiment.

Is it possible to understand Nietzsche himself as a genuine Christian thinker in this context? To the Protestant, the decisive sign of a Christian thinker is an ultimate understanding of sin, and surely Nietzsche beyond every other thinker has understood and decisively called forth the absolute impotence and the absolute perversity of a wholly fallen or repressed humanity, one overwhelmingly revealed in the uniquely modern realization of the death of God, in the wake of which the world as a whole becomes the embodiment of an absolute nothingness. Here is an enactment of the deepest possible No, but an enactment apart from which there can be no absolute Yes, and if it is Barth alone among our modern theologians who has enacted a Yes which is impossible apart from an absolute No, this enactment is far more comprehensive in Nietzsche's writing than in Barth's, and far deeper and far more dialectical, too, for it is Nietzsche and not Barth who calls forth an absolute Yes and an absolute No that are finally indistinguishable, and this is also true of both Blake and Hegel. Is this an ultimate theological truth which is finally beyond theology itself, or beyond anything that we can know as theology? Is theology itself by an innermost necessity unable to reach that faith which it claims as its ultimate ground, and therefore finally a betrayal of that ground? These are questions that have been forced upon theology, and even forced upon it by modern "atheism" itself, an atheism truly going beyond our theologies, and going beyond them in its very depth.

If we confine ourselves to the "atheisms" of Blake, Hegel, and Nietzsche, one decisive sign distinguishes them from all of our theologies, and that is their very enactment of a total Yes, a Yes which is truly all in all, but only insofar as it enacts an absolute and total No. Theologically, what is most difficult to grasp is that an absolute No to God is ultimately an absolute Yes. Already Boehme could call forth a purely negative potency in the Godhead which makes possible the divine life itself, and when that negative potency is renewed or resurrected in German Idealism it becomes actuality itself, and this also occurs in our deepest modern imaginative realizations. Nowhere else is an absolute No more fully manifest as an absolute Yes, and if it is modernity alone which has known an absolute negativity, or an absolutely actual absolute negativity, this is a pure negativity finally realizing apocalypse itself, or that apocalypse which is a final and total Yes. Just as Blake is our first fully apocalyptic poet, and Hegel our first fully apocalyptic thinker, this is an apocalypse only occurring by way of an absolute negation of God, one ecstatically recurring in Nietzsche's final apocalyptic vision, and here Nietzsche is clearly in continuity with both Blake and Hegel.

One of the most profound, if not the most profound, innovations of the Fourth Gospel is that it so purely integrates the divine movements of incarnation, crucifixion, resurrection, and apocalypse. This is a revolutionary innovation which is deeply reborn in both Blake and Hegel, but it also can be understood as being reborn in Nietzsche, too, and most clearly so in Nietzsche's enactment of the death of God as apocalypse itself. Apocalypse can only finally be known as an absolute Yes, but it is a Yes inseparable from an absolute No, and a Yes finally indistinguishable from that No. Only that No makes possible this Yes, or only crucifixion makes possible resurrection, but crucifixion is ultimately the crucifixion of God, and no one has known this more deeply than did Blake, Hegel, and Nietzsche. Yet apocalyptically crucifixion is a total Yes or a total apocalypse, an apocalypse which is all in all, one lying wholly beyond every given or manifest Western theological understanding, and yet luminously embodied in the depths of our uniquely modern "atheism," an atheism which if only thereby can be understood as a truly Christian atheism.

CHAPTER 8

Crucifixion

As I became ever more open to that revolutionary transformation of consciousness which has occurred in the modern world, I just thereby gradually became open to the possibility that a fully comparable transformation had occurred in the very genesis of Christianity. Christian theology from its beginning in Paul has known Christianity as the most ultimate of all revolutions. Indeed, it is only with the advent of Christianity that revolution itself is called forth in consciousness, for the Christian knows a truly new creation or new world which is possible only as the consequence of an apocalyptic ending of an old world. Yet it is only the most radical expressions of Christianity that can know a Christianity that has reversed itself in its very genesis. This occurs already in Paul, is present in deep sectarian expressions of Christianity, including the Radical Reformation, and is above all present in the most radical expressions of Christian thinking and vision in the modern world. While classical Protestantism cannot know such a reversal in the New Testament itself, this is called forth in modern New Testament scholarship, as clearly manifest in that paradigm which has been our dominant key in the uniquely modern quest of unearthing the authentic acts and words of Jesus, a key wherein it is precisely those words and acts which are most distant from or most challenging to the primitive churches which are most probably authentic acts and words of Jesus. Clearly such a paradigm witnesses to a reversal of Jesus in the early churches, and one which becomes overwhelmingly powerful in Hellenistic Christianity, and this is the Christianity which became orthodox Christianity in the Constantinian establishment.

It is remarkable that so few theologians have challenged Constantinian orthodoxy. This never occurs in classical Protestantism, although it deeply occurs in Milton, the deepest voice of the Radical Reformation, who gave us in *De Doctrina Christiana* perhaps our only theology which is fully biblical and fully systematic at once. But it is odd that Christian heresy was most decisively defeated by a not yet baptized Constantine and his pagan court, and that Constantine played a far greater role in the establishment of Nicene orthodoxy than did any bishop. Here the Christian can marvel indeed at a mysterious providence, and if only at this point Christian orthodoxy is unique in the religions of the world. Why such acquiescence? Why know the Roman Empire as a primary instrument of providence, an empire which undergoes a genuine metamorphosis into the Catholic Church? Is this because the Roman Empire is the most powerful empire in the history of the world? And why even after the end of Christendom is orthodoxy so powerful in Christian theology? This power is most baffling to me in New Testament scholarship itself, a scholarship commonly insisting that "kingdom" or *basilea* in the "Kingdom of God," should be translated as "rule" or "reign," as though Jesus had come to establish the imperial authority of God. The truth is that even New Testament scholarship cannot escape Constantinian orthodoxy, thereby posing the question of whether that orthodoxy can actually be transcended, and transcended in theological thinking itself.

Everyone agrees that "Kingdom of God" is the dominant if not the sole title employed by Jesus, and there is substantial agreement that this is an apocalyptic title, but what is wholly missing in our theological thinking is an actual attempt to call forth the meaning of that Kingdom of God. Here is a deep iconoclasm indeed, and one just as fully present in New Testament theology as it is in systematic theology. We know that the title "Kingdom of God" appears in no literature prior to the New Testament, not even in the Dead Sea Scrolls, where we might most expect it, so that if only here the New Testament is truly unique. So, too, is Jesus a truly new prophet in this perspective, being alone in proclaiming the immediate advent or dawning of the Kingdom of God, and there can be little doubt that this dawning is at the very center of his proclamation, and at the center of his acts and parables as well. Is a theological understanding of that dawning simply impossible? All too significantly, it is not a New Testament scholar but a historian of religions, Rudolf Otto, who has given us our fullest understanding of that dawning in *The Kingdom of God and the Son of Man*, a book studiously ignored by New Testament scholars; but so, too, do New Testament scholars commonly ignore Nietzsche's *The Antichrist*, which has given us our most radical understanding of Christianity's ultimate reversal of Jesus. Is that reversal manifest in a deep transformation of a dawning apocalyptic Kingdom of God into the pure and absolute transcendence of God?

This motif became a crucial core of my theological work, but the question arises as to how this could be an actual possibility. Is it possible to understand that the uniquely Christian God is a consequence of a profound reversal of that Kingdom of God which Jesus enacted and proclaimed? Already an understanding very close to this is present in *The Antichrist*, just as it is fully envisioned by Blake, and it was Blake who first fully rediscovered the Kingdom of God, and did so most decisively in giving us our first full imaginative enactment of the death of God (in *America*, engraved in 1793). Only a century later did New Testament scholarship recover the apocalyptic ground of the New Testament, so is it possible to think that Christianity, or the dominant expressions of Christianity, had succeeded in truly repressing Christianity's own original ground, and done so by a "forgetting" of Jesus that reminds one of Heidegger's understanding of the "forgetting" of Being? One of the most striking and original motifs of Barth's *Church Dogmatics* is its Christomonism, a Christomonism strangely paralleling an apocalyptic faith centering in the triumphant dawning of the Kingdom of God, and this despite Barth's own dogmatic repudiation of apocalypticism. Perhaps an apocalyptic theology is possible only by way of the deepest disguise, and what disguise could be greater than Christian orthodoxy itself, which only came into existence by way of a full negation of apocalypticism?

Of course, that genesis also occurred by way of a negation of Gnosticism, but Gnosticism and apocalypticism are polar twins, each revolving about an absolute world-negation, and each negating the actual worlds upon their horizons, a negation realizing for each a truly new vision of cosmic history, a cosmic history revolving about an ultimate and final fall. Gnosticism and apocalypticism are deeply contending forces in the New Testament itself, as fully manifest in Paul, but whereas a theological victory over apocalypticism occurred quickly in Christian history, the deep struggle with Gnosticism was far longer and far deeper, and many theologians believe that it is just as deep today if not deeper than it was in the ancient Christian world. It is also remarkable that deeply apocalyptic visionaries and thinkers can be identified as Gnostic in our world, as can be seen in many of the responses to both Blake and Hegel. Perhaps Gnosticism and apocalypticism are our only full contemporary mythologies, and Bultmannianism is most directed to demythologizing precisely these mythologies. Is it only a coincidence that the Dead Sea Scrolls and the Nag Hammadi scriptures were discovered simultaneously? Or is our world returning to its original ground? And, yes, returning by way of an eternal return, a return irresistible in terms of its sheer power. But is that a primordial eternal return or an apocalyptic eternal recurrence? Is it a backward or a forward movement into eternity?

These are truly exciting theological questions, and they are deeply contemporary questions. It is possible to ask if anyone can finally evade them today, and these questions have given me a passion which I cannot possibly evade or resist. Is it possible truly to be a theologian apart from an ultimate passion? One could think of Aquinas, but how much do we know about his interior life? When we think of Augustine, Luther, and Kierkegaard, we inevitably think of an ultimate and overwhelming passion. One is tempted to say that it is passion which most clearly distinguishes the theologian from the philosopher, and if only here Nietzsche is clearly a theologian and a philosopher at once. Yet one can truly be passionate only in being possessed by passion. This is a passion that every ancient thinker except Augustine could know as a curse, a curse deeply disrupting if not ending genuine thinking, and a curse that can only be overcome by a deeply disciplined thinking, a disciplined thinking that the philosopher commonly knows to be absent from theology, and it is just thereby that theology is truly groundless. Note that Spinoza can identify such passion as passivity, for it inactivates the mind, and the mind for Spinoza is the only source of true action or activity; but it is passivity or passion which is also the source of the deepest philosophical illusion, which Spinoza could know as any kind of teleological thinking, a thinking which rationally is absolutely groundless, and is the product of passivity or passion alone.

I do think that it is true that no genuine theology can negate or transcend teleological thinking, unless it does so by way of a Hegelian negation that is negation and affirmation at once, and if passion is truly the source of all teleological thinking, then passion is essential to theology. One observes that even Spinoza could not refrain from expressing joy, although this leads one to ask if a pure joy is wholly without passion, or without anything that we can recognize as passion. Yet the very word "passion" is most associated by the Christian with the Crucifixion, and certainly a thinking of that passion has always been a Christian theological obligation. But again it is remarkable how little this has occurred in Christian theology, and when it does fully occur it occurs far more deeply and comprehensively in Hegel than it does in our theologians. Is it theologically impossible to think that passion? Or, if this is attempted, does it inevitably lead to deep heresy or to deep apostasy? Here we come to that primal theological question of the role of God Himself in the Crucifixion. Is it only the humanity of Christ that suffers and dies? For the divinity of Christ in all established Christian theology is an absolute aseity that can be affected by nothing outside itself. This is the position of Aquinas (*Summa Theologica* III, 46, 12), and seemingly of every Christian orthodoxy, although here, too, Barth's orthodoxy is deeply in question.

Indeed, one wonders if it is possible to be a modern orthodox theologian at this absolutely crucial point. Already Milton was driven to Arianism by his refusal to accept a divinity of Christ that cannot and does not suffer and die. If the Passion of Christ is absolutely fundamental in the history of Christian worship and devotion, how could that not be the Passion of God, so that if Athanasius could defeat Arianism with his passionate argument that only a fully divine redeemer could possibly be a source of salvation for us, does not that salvation occur through the very passion and death of the Redeemer? We know that Christological arguments were a source of violent confrontation in the ancient Christian world, and even of civil war, so that Constantine himself could know the necessity of a legally enforced theological orthodoxy, and one that was not truly abated until well over a thousand years. While there is a seemingly comparable orthodoxy in the Islamic world, there it was never enforced so violently or so comprehensively, so that not only is Christianity the most intolerant religion in history, but its deepest and most terrible intolerance is directed solely against itself, against its own heretics, and most so against its Christological heretics. Arianism was not only long manifest as the greatest heresy, but as the source of all heresies, so that the full divinity of Christ is the deepest and most powerful of all Christian dogmas, and this is a deep theological truth which I have never truly doubted. But is it possible to affirm this truth even while affirming the uniquely Christian God, or is it possible that we can only accept the uniquely Christian Christ by accepting the death of the uniquely Christian God, and accept that death as occurring in the Crucifixion of God?

Is it possible to think such a theology? These propositions can be affirmed, but can they actually be thought, and thought in an authentically theological thinking? The truth is that these propositions have been deeply and profoundly thought. This fully occurs in Hegel's dialectical philosophy, and perhaps it is for that very reason that the theologian has so deeply opposed Hegel, and insisted that his is a philosophy negating every possible theology, and hence Hegelianism is the deepest philosophical enemy that theology has ever faced. Of course, almost a millennium ago theology faced a fully comparable enemy in Aristotelianism, and Aquinas not only fully met and absorbed this enemy, but it is possible to understand that Christianity would never have survived the Middle Ages apart from this victory. Surely the stakes are no lower for the theologian today, and even if few theologians take theology so seriously, there are few who doubt the overwhelming challenge that Christianity faces today, a challenge inseparable from a deep inquiry within Christianity itself, and this is the challenge which is most uniquely a theological challenge. Barth understood this all too fundamentally, as did Kierkegaard, too, for the exterior challenge to faith is finally most deeply an interior challenge. It is in the depths of faith that we most purely oppose faith, and most so in our very faith in God.

Both Barth and Tillich could know that faith in God finally transcends every possible belief in God, an argument most powerfully although also most elusively articulated in the *Phenomenology of Spirit*; but neither Barth nor Tillich could know Godhead itself as finally being the truest enemy of faith, even if Barth unlike Tillich could know a non-Christological Godhead as the purest enemy of faith. Naming the enemy is a genuine theological challenge, but every real theologian knows that the enemy is most deeply within, and most deeply within faith itself. Here lies that Satan who is truly the opposite of Christ, or that darkness which is truly the opposite of light, or that God who is the very opposite of every possible life. I cannot deny that I have been deeply affected by that hatred of God which so pervades late modernity, a hatred of God fully manifest in the great body of our literature, and only thinly disguised in our philosophy, a hatred of God which I could experience as a hatred of the theologian, a theologian who is the most open source of our deepest pathology. Frankly, I genuinely respect those who are repulsed by an Augustine, a Luther, or a Kierkegaard. I do believe that they are our deepest pathologists, or deepest apart from Nietzsche; yet Nietzsche truly belongs within this tradition, and many of his philosophical opponents justly recognize this identity. And these are the very thinkers who call forth the most terrible God, that God who has predestined all humanity to an eternal Hell, and only released from that inevitable destiny a tiny elect whom He has freely and gratuitously chosen, and the very Heaven given this elect is inseparable from the eternity and the sheer horror of Hell.

Surely there is no more terrible deity in the history of religions. Nietzsche knew this all too clearly, which is just why he could know the Christian God and only the Christian God as absolute No-saying and absolute No-saying alone, and in thinking that No-saying Nietzsche could think the depths of our pathology itself. Never was thinking more realistic than this, a thinking that could think the deepest depths of our darkness only by thinking the absolute No-saying of God. At this point even Hegel pales before Nietzsche, to say nothing of Kant; indeed, every previous philosopher is a genuine innocent in this perspective, and every succeeding philosopher as well. But is it possible to know an ultimate and a final darkness without knowing God, and is the very knowledge of this darkness a genuine knowledge of God? Here, we can see why even modern Thomists such as Karl Rahner can finally affirm the absolute unknowability of God, for the God who we can actually know is too terrible to contemplate, so that in this perspective there is no more dangerous or more pathological vocation than theology, a discipline that truly is a sickness unto death. Why then choose theology? Why accept such a loathsome and pathological calling? Can one here be at most simply a scapegoat? Would it not be far wiser simply to end such a calling?

Our contemporary world has very nearly succeeded in ending every genuine theological calling. Perhaps it knows all too well that theology is not truly a vocation for the healthy-minded, and I was shocked by John Cobb's wonder that I did not realize that all process theologians are once-born or healthy-minded. No, I can only finally think of theology as a vocation for the sick soul. I simply cannot imagine theological depth apart from a true opening to the deepest pathology. How could one truly know an absolute No-saying without being deeply affected by it? There is no innocent knowledge here, nor any actual understanding of innocence itself, for here innocence can only be an innocence lost. And it is most lost by our very knowledge of God! If only here we can truly know God, and most know God in actually knowing the final loss of our innocence, as every theologian knows this is precisely the point at which apologetics is most powerful, for we cannot know the actual depths of either guilt or darkness without knowing God. Kafka is an overwhelming witness here, and I simply cannot imagine how it is possible to read Kafka and not to know God, and to hear the very voice of God in this writing, a writing embodying an absolute judgment, and therefore embodying the voice of God. If only in the depths of our guilt and darkness, God is very much alive today; no one knew this more deeply than Nietzsche, which is just why his proclamation of the death of God can only truly be heard with a Yes and Amen.

Why is it not possible to understand the death of God as occurring in the Crucifixion itself? Is the sacrifice of Christ not finally the sacrifice of God? Is this why the cross is the most offensive symbol in the history of religions, one wholly unique to Christianity, and yet profoundly resisted by Christianity itself, as can be seen not only in Christian theological thinking but in Christian art and iconography (for the cross does not truly or fully appear in Christian art until almost a thousand years after the advent of Christianity)? Even Dante could not envision the Crucifixion, and when this first fully occurs in Western poetry in *Paradise Lost*, it occurs only through a revolutionary vision of both God and Christ, one in which an uncrossable chasm separates the absolute sovereignty of the Father from the humiliation, suffering, and death of the Son. This is a chasm that only deepens in the further evolution of a uniquely modern Christian vision. And when the death of God is first called forth in Western vision and thinking, in Blake and Hegel, it is inseparable from a pure vision or a pure thinking of the Crucifixion. If it was just at this point that both Blake and Hegel transcended their earlier vision and thinking, it is just here that each is most deeply offensive, and most deeply offensive to the depths of faith itself. Is not the very ultimacy of this offense a decisive sign of the presence of an ultimate faith? Is a truly profound offense possible apart from the depths of faith? Is not an ultimate offense only and wholly within?

One of the advantages of entering theology through the history of religions is that it is then possible to understand the genuine distinctiveness of Christianity, and one of the fundamental points at which Christianity is most distinct if not unique is that very transformation which Christianity has undergone in the course of its historical development. Only Buddhism rivals Christianity here, but now Buddhologists are calling forth deep continuities between Theravada and Mahayana and Vajrayana Buddhism, whereas an apprehension of such continuities have become far more difficult for historians of Christianity. Newman could understand the development of Christian doctrine as an organic and necessary historical evolution, but no such understanding has appeared in twentieth-century historiography, and above all not since the discovery of an apocalyptic ground of an original Christianity. This was the very ground which was annulled or wholly transformed in ancient Christianity, and when it is renewed in Christianity it is always renewed as a profoundly heretical movement, and never more so than in the advent of a uniquely modern apocalypticism. Both Blake and Hegel are deep expressions of this apocalypticism, and perhaps it is their very apocalypticism which is most offensive to all established faith, and overwhelmingly so since this is an apocalypticism inseparable from an enactment of the death of God.

Could anything be more offensive than an enactment of the death of God? But is this not at the very center of the ultimate offense of Christianity itself? Surely this is true of Paul, and of Luther, too, or of the young Luther, and so, too, is it true of Blake and Hegel, although here the enactment of the death of God is far more comprehensive and final than it had ever previously been. Can that be understood as the consequence of a genuine and necessary evolution of Christianity? Newman was once one of my theological masters, and I immersed myself in his work during my Catholic voyage. Indeed, I continue to believe that he is the greatest of modern Catholic theologians, and most so in his very understanding of the evolution of Christianity. This was a truly revolutionary understanding, and even if it has been reversed by great historians of dogma such as Adolf Harnack, the paradigm of theological evolution remains intact, even if now it must be the very opposite of Newman's paradigm. Certainly this is how Kierkegaard understood the history of Christianity, and Nietzsche, too; but it is also possible to understand that Christianity's reversal or inversion of its original ground is a genuine Christian evolution, and one realizing itself ever more deeply in this evolutionary transformation. This is how Hegel understood the history of Christianity, so that if Hegel could apprehend an overwhelming gulf between ancient and modern Christianity, that gulf itself is a decisive sign of a profoundly forward-moving historical realization.

Of course, Hegel understood his own philosophical system as the final culmination of this ultimate historical movement, and one comprehending not only the history of Christianity but the history of the world, and if nothing could be a greater offense, and even a philosophical offense, Hegel is the most offensive philosopher in world history; yet it is possible that his philosophy is an enactment of a uniquely Christian offense, and of a uniquely Christian universalism. The truth is that Hegel was theologically orthodox in understanding Christianity as the absolute religion, no innovation whatsoever occurs here. Hegel's profound and ultimate innovation occurs in his calling forth of a uniquely Christian movement in the depths of pure thinking itself, and yet this is a uniquely Christian movement which is simultaneously a universal movement, one that has not only historically and universally occurred, but is now open to all who are capable of pure thinking, and whose occurrence is absolutely actual even if invisible to the great body of humanity. It is remarkable how closely such thinking echoes Augustine's *City of God*, and just as it is possible to understand Hegel as a truly Augustinian thinker, he is certainly an imperialistic Christian thinker, and paradoxically is most imperialistic theologically in his very "atheism." For this is an "atheism" comprehending that truly new world which has now been born. All of us are now citizens of this new world, and all of us are consequences of a uniquely modern death of God, and therefore consequences of the Crucifixion itself.

No one has thought of God more universally than did Hegel, or no one since Augustine himself, yet Hegel became a universal thinker only in thinking the death of God. If he could know this very thinking as a rethinking of Luther, Hegel's Protestantism is Catholic and Protestant at once — Catholic in its universal horizon and Protestant in its radical thinking of justification. This is a justification which now and for the first time can be understood as occurring in the depths of thinking itself, and even in the depths of a purely logical thinking, a thinking finally thinking kenosis or self-emptying and kenosis alone. Luther could intuit that justification, but he could not think it, or purely think it, hence his assaults upon that whore "reason," assaults which Hegel could renew in his assaults upon *Verstand*. But *Verstand* is finally transcended by *Vernunft*, that purely dialectical thinking which negates and transcends every possible "reason," but only thereby does reason truly become or realize itself. And what could be a greater offense than understanding true reason as justification itself, a justification enacted in all genuine philosophical thinking? Even if this only fully occurs in the course of two and a half millennia of philosophical evolution, occur it does, for it was Hegel who created the history of Being, and this history is finally the history of justification. For Hegel knows the history of Being, or the history of God, as an ultimate and universal process of atonement or reconciliation, and one finally realized only by an apocalyptic union of the polarities or absolutely opposing poles of Godhead or Absolute Spirit.

Now the Christian knows justification as occurring only in the Crucifixion, and this is true of Hegel, too, but a uniquely Hegelian thinking universalizes the Crucifixion. This is a deep philosophical and theological innovation, and here philosophical and theological thinking are united. Never previously had philosophical and theological thinking been so purely identified, or not since the pre-Socratics, and is this why a Nietzsche or a Heidegger can so deeply center his thinking upon the pre-Socratics, and even do so in attempting to unthink Hegel? Hegel himself could claim that every fragment of Heraclitus is present in the *Science of Logic*, but, so, too, could he claim that all philosophical thinking is fully and even totally present in his system. This is surely the most audacious claim ever made in the history of philosophy, but it was Hegel who created a thinking enacting the history of philosophy, and here the history of philosophy is at bottom the history of theology, too. And this is a history not only deeply grounded in God, but revolving about the history of God in thinking itself, for here the history of Being is the history of God, and this is a history culminating in that apocalypse which is the full and final advent of Absolute Spirit or the Absolute Idea. Is it possible to think the history of God? Is this not a pure and ultimate illusion, and one with catastrophic consequences in late modernity? For innumerable scholars understand Hegelianism as a deep source of twentieth-century totalitarianism, and this was already profoundly understood by Kierkegaard himself.

Yet it is also possible to understand Christianity itself as such a source, and most clearly so a truly secularized Christianity, a secularization certainly occurring in Hegel, but therein Hegel is just as much if not far more so a witness rather than a creator, for as Kierkegaard was the first to know, Christianity has become the very opposite of itself in the modern world, and this is a deep secularization which has only occurred in a Christian world and horizon. Certainly this can be understood as the consequence of a uniquely modern realization of the death of God, but that does open the possibility that this is a uniquely modern realization of the Crucifixion itself, a crucifixion that is universalized in the very advent of modernity. For only with the birth of modernity does a true and actual atheism become possible, and not only possible but actual, an actuality that is ever more fully universalized in the very evolution of modernity. But such universalization could be understood as a universalization of the depths of Christianity itself, and the universalization of a uniquely Christian justification, a justification occurring only through the death of the uniquely Christian God. Only with the full birth of modernity can God be known as being wholly solitary and alone, the very Father of *Paradise Lost*, for only with that birth does there occur a yawning chasm between the Father and the Son, and one making impossible any genuinely modern orthodox Trinitarianism, and when one finally appears in the first volume of Barth's *Church Dogmatics*, it can only be realized by way of a profoundly backward-moving theological movement, and one reversing modernity itself.

Is that the price that must be paid for theology today? Or is an opposite choice possible, a choice accepting full modernity as a universalization of Christianity, one in deep continuity with its original ground, a continuity most openly manifest in a uniquely modern apocalypticism, and in that very apocalypticism enacting the death of God? A deeply modern apocalypticism can know the death of God as redemption itself. Is this only a perverse parody of genuine Christianity, a true reversal and inversion of Christianity itself, one which is truly Satanic in this deepest of all possible negations, and Satanic likewise in its subsequent effects? Many if not most theologians can so respond to our atheism, but they, too, pay an ultimate price, and that is a total isolation of theology from all modernity, as most purely enacted by Barth. For every middle way between an ancient faith and a modern atheism is now withering away, and as Newman could already foresee, the only real choice in full modernity is between an ancient faith and pure atheism itself. Yet what is pure atheism? Is it not inevitably a fully theological atheism, one fully present in Blake, Hegel, and Nietzsche, and an atheism present here far more profoundly and ultimately than it is in every nontheological atheism? Indeed, it is a nontheological atheism which is finally an illusion, and a truly theological atheism was already present in that Epicureanism which was the only genuine atheism in the ancient world, and if it is only the Western world which has truly known atheism, this cannot be a true or pure atheism apart from a genuine negation of God. But this is a negation which the Christian alone knows as a self-negation, and a self-negation or self-emptying occurring in the Crucifixion itself.

Yet is it that self-negation or self-emptying which calls forth the absolute transcendence of God, a pure and wholly other transcendence truly alien to the Old Testament, except for the Book of Job. Only now is it possible to know the Torah of the Old Testament as an alien Torah which is the source of sin and death, as in Paul, and even to know the God of the old covenant as Satan, as in the Fourth Gospel. An absolute world-negation first enters the world in Christianity, and just as we now can understand that Gnosticism originates in Christianity, it is Christianity which first knows the absolute No of God, or knows that No as Godhead itself. Is this a No only fully or actually released by the Crucifixion, a crucifixion realizing transcendence itself as an absolute No, and only thereby releasing or embodying the absolute

Yes of God? Now this is a Yes of God which is the consequence of an absolute sacrifice or self-emptying, and is wholly unreal apart from the self-negation of Godhead itself, a self-negation which the Christian knows as the Crucifixion. Only that self-negation calls forth a wholly other transcendence, a truly alien transcendence, one known to Israel only in the Book of Job, the most subversive book of the Old Testament, and the only writing of Israel which could know that pure transcendence which Hegel could know as the "Bad Infinite," or the only infinite which is and only is the absolute opposite of the finite.

Christian theologians can rejoice that only Christianity truly knows the absolute transcendence of God, a transcendence alien to every philosophy, except for the scholastic expressions of Neoplatonism, but the Protestant theologian knows scholasticism as a voice of the Antichrist, and above all since scholasticism claims to embody a purely theoretical knowledge of God, a knowledge which could only be a true idol, and an idol reversing the absolute transcendence of God. Now it is true that Protestantism is a consequence of a deep nominalism, a nominalism breaking asunder every scholastic integration of reason and revelation, but nominalism is an ultimate source of modernity itself, and if the God of nominalism is absolutely other as is no previous philosophical understanding of God, this can be and has been understood as an authentic recovery of the uniquely Christian God, that God who is absolute transcendence and absolute transcendence alone. Only that transcendence could be a truly alien transcendence, and while this transcendence only became conceptually and imaginatively fully manifest and real after almost two millennia of historical evolution, that evolution did occur, and with the advent of the twentieth century that evolution would appear to be truly irreversible. Is this why all philosophical thinking about God has ended in the twentieth century, or ended for all purely philosophical thinking within a Christian horizon, or all philosophical thinking in genuine continuity with our uniquely Western history?

CHAPTER 9

Ethics

At no point are the catastrophic consequences of the modern realization of the death of God more openly manifest than they are in our
ethical life and thinking. Only in late modernity is ethics itself profoundly in crisis. Now the very possibility of ethical thinking and ethical action is deeply in question, and far more so than it has ever
previously been. All genuine theologians are deeply aware of this
crisis, and so much so that in our world theology would appear to be
alive only in the ethical arena, and only here is the contemporary secular mind open to the challenge of theology. Is this a challenge that can
be met? Of course, overwhelming problems are posed by Christian
ethics itself, and most dramatically for me by Albert Schweitzer, our
only twentieth-century theologian who can be known as a saint. For it
was Schweitzer far more than any other New Testament scholar who
demonstrated the total irrelevance of the ethics of Jesus, decisively
calling them forth as an interim ethics only real by way of the immediate advent of the Kingdom of God, and yet it was in obedience to the
purely apocalyptic Jesus that Schweitzer accepted his missionary calling. Schweitzer also demonstrated, and most profoundly in his great
book on Paul, that Christian ethics loses its authentic and radical foundation when it is divorced from apocalypticism. This is just what
occurs in ancient Christianity, and already so in the New Testament
itself, as above all manifest in the Fourth Gospel. Now even if it is
true that Christianity again and again recovered a radical ethical
ground, it did so only in its most radical expressions, all of which were
directed against the very power of the world, a power here manifest as
the very opposite of the power of Christ.

It would be difficult to deny that it is Marxism which has released the deepest ethical passion in the modern world, and even if this is fully capable of being transformed into its very opposite, this has occurred continually in Christianity, and most so in those very periods when Christianity was most powerful and most unchallengeable. Marxism has commonly been theologically identified as a Christian heresy, and above all so in its apocalypticism; but Marxism arose at the very time of the ending of Christendom, leading many Christians to choose Marxism or Communism as the new church, and a universal church which is the destiny of all humanity. Marxism most affected theology in its purely negative thinking, a thinking directed against all established or "given" reality, but this is a dialectical thinking intending an absolute reversal of the given, and so it could be understood theologically as being in genuine continuity with authentic Christian thinking. Certainly Marxism is a profoundly subversive thinking, but so, too, is theological thinking in its truest expressions, and no one assaulted or subverted the ancient world more deeply than did Augustine. Marxism is perhaps most ambivalent in its relation to Hegelianism, for it is at once a genuine expression of Hegelianism and yet the deepest subversion of Hegelianism, apart from Kierkegaard and Nietzsche, and it is the truly non-Hegelian expressions of Marxism such as Stalinism and Maoism which have been its most demonic and totalitarian expressions.

One ultimate ethical problem which Marxism exposes is antinomianism, and a historical antinomianism, an antinomianism directed against every historical law and authority, one echoing both the prophets of Israel and the prophets of Taoism. For antinomianism is inseparable from every genuine prophetic revolution, and it is reborn in every truly prophetic enactment, as we can see most clearly in modernity in the prophetic vision of Blake. So, too, we encounter a profound antinomianism in Nietzsche. Nowhere else are Blake and Nietzsche so truly united, but this is a union that they also share with Marx, and it is only Marxism which has embodied a universal antinomianism, one posing the greatest revolutionary challenge that has ever occurred historically. Or does such a challenge occur in the very advent of Christianity, and is this the challenge that historical Christianity has most deeply subverted or reversed? Nietzsche and Kierkegaard could share a fundamental understanding of such a subversion, so is it possible that subversion itself is a true key unlocking the mystery of the genesis of Christianity? Blake, Kierkegaard, and Nietzsche could all understand historical Christianity as becoming the very opposite of Jesus or the incarnate Christ. Obviously this could only occur by way of a deep subversion, but is that subversion manifest in Christian ethics, or in our dominant Christian ethics, or in our ethical consciousness itself?

Theologians have been most effective in the ethical arena in drawing forth the deeply destructive consequences of every pure imperative, or every imperative wholly divorced from the indicative, or every imperative which is "law" and law alone. A Bultmannian demythologizing is perhaps most powerful in its demonstration of the identity of the imperative and the indicative in the deeper expressions of the New Testament, and such an identity is already present in post-exilic prophecy, as most fully manifest in Second Isaiah. This is surely an ultimate ground of prophetic antinomianism, one which is shared by both Paul and the Fourth Gospel, and if only here the Fourth Gospel can be known as an apocalyptic gospel. How could this be? Is it possible that a deep subversion of apocalypticism could be a genuine expression of apocalypticism? And could this be said of historical Christianity itself? Christianity is deeply paradoxical in so fully embodying an absolute negation of the world with an absolute affirmation of the world, and if this is most true theologically in ancient Christianity in Augustine himself, it nowhere occurs more concretely than in the ethical arena, for Christianity has simultaneously been a profound challenge to the world and a profound submission to the world, at once the most worldly major religion and yet the most otherworldly religion, and nowhere more so than in its ethical thinking and praxis.

One has only to read the fourth volume of Barth's *Church Dogmatics* to realize how deeply worldly even the deepest Christian ethics can be. Yet this is clearly an "otherworldly" ethics, and even if it embodies the deepest affirmations of an ancient and paternalistic authority, it nevertheless subverts that authority, and most subverts it insofar as it calls forth an ethics whose first principle is that there is no humanity outside the humanity of Jesus Christ. Our contemporary historical understanding of Jesus is centered upon Jesus the revolutionary, and just as this understanding has been truly even if only indirectly affected by Marxism, we find it virtually impossible to

understand a genuinely revolutionary thinking which is not in some
genuine sense a Marxist thinking, and while this no doubt played a
crucial role in the genesis of the most conservative society in late
modernity, this is a society which genuinely can be known as a truly
"aethical" society, and the first such society in history. Already a truly
aethical or transethical world was manifest when I was a young theologian. This alone appeared to make ethical thinking either unreal or
utopian. Then as now Buddhist ethics could be manifest as a real
ethics precisely in its very "unreality," and so, too, apocalyptic ethics
can then be called forth as a real ethics, and most real in its very
grounding in the end of the world. Schweitzer is not alone in deeply
understanding this. He could rather be thought of as belonging to a
genuine company of modern apocalyptic thinkers, thinkers and visionaries who have simultaneously deeply unthought and deeply rethought
ethics itself.

How does one find a way into this ethics? First, it is clearly vastly
distant from all of our established ethics, and so much so that it can
only be an antinomian ethics, an ethics subverting every established
ethical principle, and subverting it even by reversing it, as can concretely be observed in both Blake's and Nietzsche's reversal of the
Decalogue. It is very odd, indeed, that the Decalogue could have
become known as a universal ethical law, a Decalogue originating in a
unique covenant of Yahweh with Israel, and a Decalogue inseparable
in the Bible from Torah, a uniquely Israelitic "law," and so much so
that Jewish scholars can truly demonstrate that such a law is unknown
in Christianity. But it is only the Christian form of the Decalogue that
Blake and Nietzsche can so deeply attack, a Decalogue or "thou shalt"
and "thou shalt not" which is and only is a pure and absolute imperative, hence a Decalogue truly absent from Judaism, but also absent
from both Hinduism and Islam, so perhaps this is a uniquely Christian
"law." Such an understanding of the law can be known as having a
genuine source in Paul, and while absent in Augustine, it certainly
occurs or recurs in Luther, and is given its purest philosophical expression in Kant, and if this was a true philosophical innovation, this is a
reflection of a deep historical transformation, a historical transformation in which the indicative and the imperative become truly divorced
and truly alienated and estranged from each other.

Such a condition can be understood as an ultimate condition of the late ancient world, just as it can be understood as a condition making possible the genesis of apocalypticism itself, but the apparent ending of apocalypticism in both rabbinic Judaism and the Catholic Church does not finally end this condition, for it is reborn again and again in both Islamic and Christian apocalypticism, and we must never forget Luther's deep apocalyptic ground. Only that ground makes possible Luther's understanding of the dominance of Satan in our world, an understanding that had already occurred in Dante, and would be reborn in both Milton and Blake, and if this is a dominant motif in a uniquely Christian epic, that is an epical enactment calling forth a profound ethical transformation, and one only possible by way of the most ultimate negation. It fascinates me that Christian ethical thinkers can be so indifferent to the Christian epic. Is there anywhere else where we can discover such a pure vision of an ultimate ethical transformation, or even discover an ethics so deeply engaged with its own world? My Stony Brook colleague, David Erdman, demonstrated in his marvelous book *Blake: Prophet Against Empire* that virtually every one of Blake's images was directed to and against a true historical actuality of his world, and just as this is also largely true of both Dante and Milton, it makes fully manifest an ethical language which is a truly embodied language, and embodied in the full actualities of history itself, as is no philosophical or theological language, or none apart from Nietzsche.

But the Christian epic is also a truly and ultimately apocalyptic epic. Here ethical enactment and apocalyptic enactment are inseparable, and if this makes possible the deepest negation, this is a truly ethical negation, one releasing a profound ethical affirmation, only possible in the depths of the world itself, and in the depths of that world that is actually at hand. Antinomianism is also powerful in the Christian epic, and as that epic evolves, so, too, does its antinomianism. While it is minimal in Dante, it is major in Milton, who deeply believed that Christ had ended the authority of the moral law, and then it is overwhelming in Blake, who could envision every law as the Law of Urizen or Satan. Yet for both Blake and Milton it is the very ending or transcendence of all moral law which releases the truest ethical engagement, or the deepest ethical action. Only that ending makes possible what Blake knows as "self-annihilation," and only that ending makes possible what Milton knows as a true and truly individual obedience to Christ. Long before Nietzsche and Freud, Milton and Blake know law as the source of repression, and the deeper the law the deeper the repression, hence the necessity of the reversal of the "Decalogue," or a uniquely Christian Decalogue, a Decalogue whose pure imperative is an absolute authority, and the absolute authority of God. That authority is first imaginatively reversed in *Paradise Lost*, a reversal most deeply occurring here in the very kenotic movement of the Son of God. That movement has a full parallel in the ultimately downward movement of Satan, and it is the absolute opposition between Satan and the Messiah which is here the very arena of ethical engagement and life.

What is most missing from modern theological ethics, and perhaps modern philosophical ethics as well, is any real opening to our actual historical world, a world in which ethics is seemingly impossible, but Max Weber established an ethical thinking seemingly the opposite of this. Weber had a fundamental impact upon my thinking, and most so in his unique understanding of Calvinism and an "inner-worldly" asceticism. Thereby Calvinism can be understood to have truly transcended its origin in Calvin and a theocratic Geneva, but as Weber knew, it never loses its ground in an absolute predestination; yet here predestination is embodied in historical actuality itself, and even embodied in the very secularization of Christianity. Only Weber in the twentieth century has given us a fundamental understanding of secularization. Here, as elsewhere, Weber is a deep Hegelian and a deep Marxist at once. Here, too, we discover an ultimate "cunning of reason," a providential or necessary and inevitable history, but one now culminating in the very reversal of its original ground, a culmination enclosing us within an "iron cage." It is Weber above all others who has given us an ethical understanding of our historical prison house, and just as Weber stands alone as a sociologist of the world religions, he stands alone in giving us a genuinely ethical understanding of actual historical worlds. Indeed, Weber could understand that a truly inner-worldly asceticism is a genuine expression of faith, one releasing a full and pure action in the world, and a truly pragmatic action, just as he could understand that the prophetic revolution was made possible by what he termed the "psychic economy" of the prophets, wherein all the energy of the prophet is directed to a demand for action rather than mythical vision or understanding, a pure action that is total obedience to Yahweh.

While Weber himself was broken by his own work, thereby allowing us a glimpse of its ultimate power, and even demonic power, his work does give us something like a sanctification of the forbidden, a theological justification of secularization, and one occurring in the realization that it is precisely a comprehensive secularization that releases the deepest energy, and one occurring not only in modern Calvinism but in ancient Confucianism. Thereby we can see that these are the driving forces in modernity, and forces which are most powerful when they are most theologically disguised. Genuine Calvinism, in this sense, is truly an invisible religion, or a profoundly secularized faith, and it is precisely as such that it is most powerful, but here is a power inseparable from an ultimate confidence. This can be understood as an eschatological or apocalyptic confidence, one only possible as a consequence of the awesome threat of damnation or an eternal darkness, and no one has had a deeper understanding of a *horror religiosus* than Weber, and while no one can know whether he or she is redeemed, the very impossibility of this knowledge releases pure action itself. For this is a paradoxical impossibility: our very ignorance of our own ultimate destiny is inseparable from a certainty of an ultimate providence, a hidden providence which is predestination, and precisely thereby an absolute and total providence.

Even the Marxist knows such a providence, and could not be a Marxist apart from the absolute providence or the absolute necessity of history itself, yet this is an absolute necessity impelling an absolute action, as Spinoza already knew, and while many can know our world as a totally pragmatic world, it is certainly not pragmatic in either Marx's or Weber's sense, for theirs is a pragmatism that can act only by turning the world upside down. Is this a truly new ethics? Or is it the renewal of an ancient prophetic ethics? Both could be true, of course, if an ancient prophetic ethics had truly been forgotten in full modernity, and why is there so little awareness of the forgetting of ethics? Have we not forgotten ethics more deeply than we have forgotten Being? Yes, Levinas knows this, and Kafka, too, even as Spinoza knew it at the very beginning of modern philosophy, but these are thinkers who think within the horizon of the Torah. Is such thinking possible for the Christian theologian? Can we understand true action itself as an antinomian action, one released from every obedience to the law, or released from everything historically knowable as "law"? And if the Torah of Israel is a profoundly aniconic law, it, too, could have been reborn in our history, but only insofar as it is open to a total secularization. But can that secularization in its very religious or ultimate antinomianism be a genuine rebirth of the Bible?

Here, as elsewhere, the Christian subverts the Torah of Israel, but here a Christian subversion is most deeply a subversion of a uniquely Christian law, just as it is the subversion of an absolute and total authority whose only full epiphany is in the uniquely Christian God. Yet this is a subversion releasing a new life, and while this new life is inseparable from a new and even apocalyptic ending, the ending which it most decisively knows is the ending of authority itself. Such an ending is inescapable in every full antinomianism, but is it inescapable in the fullest expressions of our ethical life and engagement, or in our fullest openings to humanity and the world? Are such openings possible apart from an ultimate sense of providence or necessity, or apart from what theologically can be known as predestination, a predestination which is the consequence of a free grace and a free grace alone, and thus is absolutely independent of our choice or power? In this perspective, it is moral discipline which most turns one away from grace, just as it is moral judgment which most disengages us from every actual opening to another, and "morality" itself which is a true prison, and a prison in which the "law" itself is our warden, as Kafka so deeply knew. Then the absolute authority of the pure imperative is an absolutely enclosing authority, one imprisoning us in its iron cage, then all deep assurance vanishes, and we can only say No. Yet predestination can know even the most terrible judgment as a liberating judgment, one liberating in its total disenactment of everything that we can know as law, but one assuring us that even the most ultimate horror of an absolute No is finally an absolute and total Yes, and in hearing that Yes we are released into pure action or pure engagement itself.

It is seldom understood that a pure predestination is an ultimate shattering of every possible law, or of everything that we can know or understand as law, hence predestination is profoundly antinomian, and most antinomian when it speaks in the name of an absolute Law. Then the Law is totally shattered as "law," but that shattering releases us from every legal authority, so that the royalist enemies of the Puritans could know predestination as the most ultimate assault upon all constituted or legal authority, and upon all human or historical authority as well. Only here does an absolute assault upon all legal and historical authority occur, so that predestination is an absolute antinomianism, and one that Weber could understand as the driving force of modernity itself. While Dante, Milton, and Blake all assaulted predestination, they nevertheless enacted it in their revolutionary epics, and most openly enacted it in their assaults upon the church, a church that has reversed predestination in its absolute laws, and most openly so in its absolute claims to temporal power and authority, claims which Dante was the first to assault profoundly, and he could understand these claims as the very voice of Satan. In *Paradise Lost* the only absolute law is the Law of the Father, but the Son breaks or transcends that Law in the atonement, and only in His response to the Son's announcement of his decision to effect that atonement does the Father recognize the majesty of the Son to be equal to His own. This antinomianism becomes total in Blake, and it becomes total in an apocalyptic history that is a totally lawless and therefore chaotic history, but that is precisely the history in which an ultimate necessity or predestination is enacted.

Every full philosophy of history is a theology of predestination, a predestination which is an absolute historical necessity, so that to understand that necessity is to understand predestination, and so likewise to enact that necessity is to enact predestination, so that not only are Hegel and Marx both philosophers of predestination, but here Marx is the purer philosopher of predestination, for he can know genuine understanding as being inseparable from praxis, and thus can know a true understanding of history as an enactment of history, and as an enactment of that absolute necessity which is absolute predestination. Only by truly conjoining Marx and Hegel could Weber reach his revolutionary understanding of secularization, a secularization in which predestination becomes an inner-worldly and not an otherworldly predestination, and only thereby making possible that truly new assurance or truly new certainty which alone makes possible a total action in the world.

Weber understood that it was a unique historical condition that made possible the full birth of an inner-worldly asceticism. For the first time in history there was an unprecedented inner isolation of the individual, so that the individual whom God has eternally damned is removed not only from all ancient religion but from all institutions as well, and thereby for the first time the individual confronts an absolute responsibility. Only this responsibility makes possible the advent of pure action itself, one which is a truly ethical engagement, but an action only possible on the foundation of an ultimate assurance, an assurance wholly independent of every possible moral character or will, and it is only the disengagement or disenactment of the moral will which releases pure action, a disenactment and disengagement which is a pure antinomianism, and hence an assault upon every possible moral action or response. Consequently, in this perspective the "moral" and the "ethical" are truly in contradiction with each other, but here language fails us, for we have no words in any of our languages to express this meaning of the "moral" and the "ethical." Yet this lacuna is not a meaningless surd, for it is called forth again and again in our history, and for the Christian it concretely calls forth our forgetting of Jesus. Have we truly forgotten that overwhelming offense which Jesus certainly evoked, and an offense most deeply occurring to those who most fully know the "Law" of God, hence an offense most ultimately occurring in and to faith itself? Is the way for which Jesus calls truly separable from that offense, or is the "ethics" of Jesus possible apart from the most ultimate offense, an offense to everything which we can possibly understand as "ethics," yet also an offense to everything which we can understand as "morality" itself?

While the form of the Sermon on the Mount is a construct of the Gospel of Matthew, it can nonetheless be accepted as the clearest and most decisive New Testament articulation of the ethics of Jesus, and it has been accepted as such throughout Christian history. But this is a truly radical ethics, indeed, one seemingly impossible to enact, and yet its language clearly calls for an actual obedience. Only Schweitzer's interpretation of this ethics makes it resolutely clear, but then it becomes impossible for all save the original Christians, for then it is absolutely inseparable from the immediate advent of the Kingdom of God. But this interpretation does give us an ethics ending every distinction between the imperative and the indicative, for then the revolutionary words of Jesus, "be perfect," are inseparable from their horizon in the immediate advent of the Kingdom of God, an advent

that will give us that "perfection," and if we follow more recent interpretations of the eschatological language of Jesus, wherein the Kingdom even now is dawning, this ultimate obedience, so far from being
a response to an absolute imperative, is a response to that indicative
which even now is overwhelmingly present. Thus the imperative is the
indicative even as the indicative is the imperative, and if this ends
everything that we can understand as ethics, it gives us a way which is
actuality itself, an actuality which is the advent or dawning of the
Kingdom of God.

Here, too, we can see how absurd are all those interpretations
which understand the Kingdom of God as the Rule or Reign of God,
and even if these dominate New Testament scholarship, at no other
point is our New Testament scholarship more truly nontheological.
But is a theological ethics actually possible? Or actually possible as an
ethics which is in genuine continuity with the ethics of Jesus? First,
we can see that it is deeply problematic if this has ever occurred in the
church, or occurred therein apart from its most radical circles, and if
we can understand movements such as the radical or "spiritual" Fran-
ciscans as recovering the ethics of Jesus, these very movements are
judged to be deeply heretical by the church. Second, we can see that
the ethics of Jesus is profoundly alien to all of our established philosophical ethics, and if Kant seemingly most purely recovered this
ethics in his understanding of the categorical imperative, that is an
understanding which we can apprehend as being most distant from the
ethics of Jesus. Third, we are coming to understand that the ethics of
Jesus is far closer to Buddhist ethics than to any established form of
Western ethics, and if only thereby we can realize that a radical
rethinking of ethics itself is now inescapable. But that rethinking is
clearly inseparable from a rethinking of theology itself, and above all
a rethinking of "God," and here a rethinking of what Jesus could possible have meant in his seemingly spontaneous evocations of God.

Is it possible that those evocations are always and at bottom evocations of the Kingdom of God? Unfortunately, New Testament scholars can give us little assistance here if only because they are now
commonly so indifferent to all such questions, but if it is possible to
answer this question affirmatively, or, to the extent that it is possible to
answer it affirmatively, then theological ethics itself acquires a truly
new meaning. Although one surely known to Schweitzer, it is wholly

absent from our theological ethics, and from our systematic theology as well, and absent because both this ethics and this theology are fully non-apocalyptic, or even anti-apocalyptic. Throughout my theological work I have known theological ethics as a true enemy, often thinking that professional ethicists are either fools or knaves, and most so in their most openly ethical language. Certainly real thinking is absent from our theological ethics, or, when it occurs, as in Barth, it is deeply conservative or reactionary, and despite its intentions therein allied with the most reactionary forces in our society, as is clearly manifest in the role of religion in reactionary movements throughout the world. Surely our political pragmatists are wise in hoping to keep religion asleep or withdrawn in our world, and it is significant that ethicists are only actually heard when they speak in the most technical fields such as medical ethics, and virtually never heard when they speak in the human arena itself.

We can understand that a pure assurance is wholly embodied in the Buddhist way, and even if this is an assurance inseparable from a dissolution or inactivation of all selfhood, it is nevertheless an ultimate assurance, and here it does parallel the way of Jesus. There is an ultimate confidence present in what we can understand as the most authentic words and acts of Jesus, and if these are inseparable from the dawning of the Kingdom of God, that Kingdom is not only the source of ultimate hope, but of an ultimate assurance, and an assurance which is certainty itself. And this is a certainty releasing the deepest engagement, an engagement which is a reversal of the values and laws of its own world, but that very reversal is an expression of certainty itself, a certainty that is the deepest possible assurance, and an assurance which is a response to or a reflection of that Kingdom of God which Paul could know as even now becoming all in all. Schweitzer's great book on Paul ends every real distinction between the ethics of Jesus and the ethics of Paul, and this is most clearly true inasmuch as each is a purely and fully apocalyptic ethics, hence an ethics inseparable from an apocalyptic and total Yes, and that is a Yes being enacted even now, so that we are not called upon to "obey" this Yes, but rather to enact it, and to enact it as that which is most immediately and actually at hand. Only an ultimate assurance and an ultimate certainty make this possible, and a certainty not in "God," but rather in that Kingdom of God which now and only now is actuality itself.

As always, our most powerful theology is a negative theology, and a purely negative theology, one here assaulting every manifest meaning of ethics itself. Hence a genuinely theological ethics is inseparable from an antinomian ethics, an antinomian ethics annulling or reversing every possible law, yet it is precisely the deepest antinomianism which releases the purest assurance. But if we can understand such assurance as being absolutely necessary to real action or real engagement, then we can understand it as a reflection of that indicative which is indistinguishable from the true imperative. This could only be an imperative not coming from the beyond, not coming from "God," but arising from immediate actuality itself. So that genuine assurance or genuine certainty is in no sense either hope or "faith," but is far rather an ultimate acceptance or an ultimate Yes-saying to that which is most immediately and actually real. Thereby we can understand how this is a Yes-saying that not only can but must undergo an ultimate and comprehensive "secularization," a secularization which theologically can be understood as an incarnational movement, and precisely thereby a movement reversing "God," or reversing that God who is pure transcendence and pure transcendence alone. Can we assert that the ethics of Jesus is one making impossible that God, and that we most deeply forget the ethics of Jesus by remembering or recalling or renewing God?

This does make manifest the ultimate question of whether or not it is possible to know God in enactment itself, or in pure action or pure act. Is that an act ending every apprehension of God, and doing so in the pure immediacy of pure act itself? This does bring a new meaning to a purely ethical engagement or ethical act, one which Weber surely understood in his radical understanding of secularization; but thereby Weber joins hands with Nietzsche, too, for it is Nietzsche who most decisively understood how pure enactment could only be an enactment of the death of God. Yet this is an enactment only historically possible within a Christian horizon, a horizon not only knowing the Crucifixion as the one source of redemption, but knowing a repetition or renewal of the Crucifixion as the deepest possible praxis, the deepest possible act or enactment. Is that an enactment already present in Jesus's ethical call, a call to self-negation or self-emptying, and one which is not simply a response to but an embodiment of that Kingdom of God which even now is dawning? This could not possibly be understood as obedience, and certainly not as an obedience to any possible law; for here the imperative wholly disappears, or is manifest only as an imperative which is indistinguishable from the indicative itself, and therefore an imperative which is the very opposite of "law," and hence the very opposite of the Law of God. Paul understood this profoundly, and if Paul created Christian theology, it is precisely at this point that our theology has most deeply reversed Paul, and done so most purely in its very knowledge of God.

This is a knowledge which must be reversed in any genuinely Christian theological ethics today. Barth understood this in his own way by understanding the theological necessity of the dissolution of every possible philosophical theology, but a philosophical theology is manifest in Barth's explicitly ethical writing, a writing evoking the absolute authority of God, and the absolute authority of that God who is the absolute or categorical imperative, so that the older Barth reminds one of the Plato of the *Laws* and of the Hegel of the *Philosophy of Right*. Must theological ethics of necessity be a deeply conservative ethics in our world? But surely such conservatism is a universe removed from Jesus himself, hence here we must forget Jesus if we are to be capable of an ethical theology, and that forgetting of Jesus is not new, it is in deep continuity with the overwhelming body of Christian tradition. Therefore such ethics is truly orthodox, and most orthodox in its very forgetting of Jesus. Nietzsche was not alone in regarding the theologian as the purest enemy of any possible act or enactment, and if he could know theology as being capable of No-saying and of No-saying alone, this is a No-saying which is the source of the deepest possible "other." Hence it is the source of *ressentiment*, and of that *ressentiment* which is the ultimate source of all repression. Thus it is the source of the deepest barriers between us, barriers which can never be crossed apart from its dissolution, but barriers which are dissolved in pure act or pure enactment itself.

Yet pure act is a wholly spontaneous and immediate act, one wholly without an intention or goal, a truly purposeless act, and only thereby can it be a truly immediate enactment. If the Kingdom of God is absolutely other than everything that is given or manifest as world, the enactment of the Kingdom of God nevertheless does not occur in heaven or the beyond. It occurs here and now! So that the ancient church, and most purely Augustine himself, in understanding the Kingdom of God as a wholly spiritual and wholly heavenly kingdom, profoundly subverted and reversed Jesus's own enactment of the Kingdom of God. Then ethics can only be a "spiritual" or other-worldly ethics, one confined to the City of God as opposed to the City of Man. If Dante revolutionized Augustinian thinking in his vision of the equality of the empire and the church, that is a truly apocalyptic vision as Augustine's is not, and one calling forth an ultimate action in the world itself. So that in Book III of *De Monarchia* Dante formulates two ultimate goals (*in duo ultima*), goals corresponding to two forms of beatitude, as opposed to the one and only eternal beatitude which is the orthodox doctrine of the church. Nothing was a more fundamental ground of Augustine's thinking than an eternal beatitude. He could most oppose an ancient cyclical thinking because it threatens the eternity of this beatitude, but this is the very beatitude which is ever more finally reversed in the history of modernity. Yet that history does ever more fully release an ultimate action, even if that action culminates in an iron cage.

The decisive question for us is how to act in our iron cage, or is genuine action possible for us? The late Weber spoke of the fate of our age as a coming polar night of icy darkness and severity, and could even know this age of total reaction as having already closed in upon us. Is our final destiny only a pure and ultimate passivity? The very words "thou shalt" evoke for us a call to such a passivity, and Nietzsche was not alone in responding to the ethical language of his world as a truly demonic or self-lacerating language, an ultimate motif virtually universal in late modern literature; so that at least in our world an ethical language can be known as a Satanic language, and Satanic in its very repressive power. A shattering of that language could open a way to liberation, yet now a liberation only possible in the darkest of all worlds, and therefore a darkness which is truly a repetition of an ancient apocalyptic darkness. But that darkness is precisely the arena of an apocalyptic enactment, and one releasing the depths of action in the depths of darkness itself. One must never forget that a tiny Jewish apocalyptic sect did transform the world, and even if it transformed the world only by transforming itself, nevertheless apocalypticism here and elsewhere demonstrates its enormous power, even its absolute power, one which is truly understood by both Marx and Hegel, both of whom could know an apocalyptic negativity as a revolutionary negativity, and most openly revolutionary in its absolute acts or enactments.

So that if absolute acts which are apocalyptic acts are the source of our iron cage, does not the recognition of such an apocalyptic ground of our imprisonment imprison us all the more? Or does it open the possibility of genuine action within our cage? Here, we are offered little if any guidance by our philosophers, who have realized a vacuum for us that is entered only by our great artists, and here the most obvious challenge is the challenge of *Finnegans Wake* itself, our final epic and our final wake, and if this work is the fullest realization of our unconscious which has ever occurred in any work, its dreamers are vibrantly awake, and most awake in the pure immediacy of their language, a language calling forth not only a universal humanity, but a humanity that is overwhelming in its language, and here pure language *is* pure act. But it is so only when we can least understand it, only when it is most distant from all understanding and all actual comprehension. Hence the necessity of this radically new language; yet even if we cannot understand it, we truly hear it, and hear it above all as enactment, a purely immediate enactment ending every barrier which is present upon its horizon, and only thereby can it culminate in its ecstatic Yes. Written at the time of our final ending, within the shadow of the Holocaust itself, and both recording and enacting a darkness more comprehensive than any other which has been called forth, the *Wake* is nevertheless a joyous wake, and most manifestly joyous in its very language and speech, as for the first time text is inseparable from speech itself; and if that speech continually speaks an absolute assault and No, it nonetheless evokes an ultimate Yes in that No, and its final word is Yes and only Yes, and even a Yes in and to this very No.

CHAPTER 10

Predestination

Nothing could have been more alien to my earlier theological thinking than a centering upon predestination, and this center arrived as an unexpected and uninvited guest. It came first as a deep offense, perhaps the deepest possible theological offense, and an offense seemingly making impossible theological thinking itself. Why an offense? Quite simply because it so ultimately assaults any possible subject of thinking, dissolving every possible interior or individual ground of that subject, and doing so by its affirmation of the absolute sovereignty of grace, a sovereignty which is all in all. Of course, such an offense occurs in Augustine, Luther, Calvin, and Barth, and perhaps ultimately even in Aquinas himself. So, too, I had become persuaded that predestination is inseparable from any full and genuine philosophy or theology of history, and that it is simply impossible to understand our Western history without understanding predestination. Yet predestination is most deeply an interior offense, one assaulting every possible individual freedom, and every possible integrity or wholeness of consciousness, thereby effecting an absolute negation if not reversal of humanity itself. Nonetheless, predestination is not fate, it is wholly different from every possible positivism or reductionism, and this because it knows an ultimate responsibility of the predestined, a responsibility whereby we are totally guilty by way of an original and universal fall, and we repeat or renew that fall in every negative or evil act. True, that repetition is irresistible to us, and so far from being a conditioned repetition, this repetition is a truly willed one, as first unveiled in Paul's Epistle to the Romans, for our wills are divided at their very center, and so much so, that as Augustine discovered, the actual freedom of our will is inseparable from the ultimate impotence of our will. Indeed, the very discovery of the freedom of the will in Paul is a discovery of the slavery of the will, and only in the dogma of predestination is that dichotomy of the will purely realized.

Nevertheless, the question arises as to how it is humanly or interiorly possible to know predestination. How is it possible to know that one's individual freedom is ultimately an illusion, or that one's purest acts are predestined acts, or that God is that absolute sovereignty comprehending every act whatsoever? A contrary question would be, how is it possible truly to know God without knowing predestination? Of course, ancient philosophy could seemingly know God without knowing predestination, but if only for this reason innumerable theologians have insisted that ancient philosophy does not truly or actually know God, and cannot know God because it cannot know revelation. Yet is it possible to know revelation or to be open to revelation without incorporating an ultimate wounding, an assault upon our deepest center, one absolutely debilitating in its overwhelming power, and most debilitating to our most integral or most interior power? There is a very good reason why the very word "God" is so circumscribed in our world, almost never pronounced by those who are wisest among us, and then only all too indirectly or elusively. In a genuine sense this is our most forbidden word, so that a truly new iconoclasm is pervasive among us, and most pervasive among those who are seemingly most distant from God. Yet the theologian, too, is reluctant to pronounce the name of God in our world, or the serious theologian, and I suspect that I have been most offensive to my fellow theologians in so frequently evoking God.

One of the ultimate paradoxes in our Western history is that predestination and freedom have been so deeply conjoined, and this is true not only of Paul and Augustine but also of Hegel and Nietzsche, and while this is a uniquely Christian paradox, it has full counterparts in Buddhism and Islam, just as it does in every genuine thinking of freedom. Thus predestination can be understood as necessity, but only as a historical rather than a natural necessity; thereby freedom itself is understood as freedom and destiny at once, and a freedom impossible apart from the actualities of history. Accordingly, this is a freedom alien to every possible innocence, or every possible primordial condition. Hence it occurs only in what the Christian knows as a wholly fallen condition, and here freedom can actually occur or be realized only through grace. Nothing is more primal for Paul than his insistence that if justification comes through the law, then Christ died for nothing (Galatians 2:21). Only the death of Christ is the source of justification or reconciliation, so that we are justified only by "his blood" (Romans 5:9), and we are united with Christ in a death like his, wherein our "flesh" or Old Adam is crucified with him, so that we might no longer be enslaved to sin, for whoever has died with Christ is freed from sin (Romans 6:5–11). Thus justification is only by grace, and by the grace of Christ, and by the grace of that Christ who was crucified for us.

Here, we can discover the deep ground of a uniquely Christian predestination, for if justification is only by grace, then it is wholly and absolutely beyond our own power. As Aquinas himself remarks, no one has been so mad as to hold that our merits were the cause of God's predestining the elect; it is God's will alone that is the source of predestination, therefore the foreknowledge of merits is not the motive or reason of predestination, and yet what is from freedom and what is from grace are not distinct, for that which occurs through our free will also occurs from predestination (*Summa Theologica* I, 23, 5). Paul is here Aquinas's primary source, for this predestination is unthinkable apart from the Crucifixion, that one source of an absolutely undeserved grace, and a grace unveiling our ultimately fallen condition. By knowing this grace we can know that it occurs only in the depths of our fallenness, and thus to think the Crucifixion is to know the absolute sovereignty of grace, a grace which we name with the name of election or predestination. It is precisely when Crucifixion is unthought that predestination is unthought as well; hence it is not accidental that predestination is so absolutely primal in Augustine, Luther, Calvin, and Barth, and so deeply absent in those very theologians who do not think the Crucifixion. In one sense, the theological ground of predestination is extraordinarily simple, but in another sense it is extraordinarily complex, so it is that Barth is virtually alone as a theologian of predestination since the Reformation. Inevitably, Barth is also alone as a truly modern theologian in knowing the absolute No of God, and only that

No makes possible the predestination of the damned, a predestination apart from which the predestination of the elect is wholly illusory, as affirmed by every theologian of predestination.

Here is the supreme scandal of Christianity, one deeply offending everyone. Barth could profoundly transform this scandal with his unique doctrine that it is only Christ who suffers damnation, but thereby he deepens the inseparability of damnation and redemption. If we can only know redemption by knowing the Crucifixion, we thereby know the absolute No of God, and we can truly know that No only in Christ, and only in the Crucifixion itself. Yet can we think the Crucifixion without thinking the death of God? Here Barth's Christomonism is most precarious, for how can we think the totality of God in Christ without thinking the death of God? We can see here a genuine reason why Christian theology has so overwhelmingly known an ultimate distinction between the humanity and the divinity of Christ, one wherein only the humanity and not the divinity of Christ suffers passion and death, hence the orthodox condemnation of patripassionism. But that very condemnation confines the sacrifice of Christ to his humanity alone, leading to the inevitable conclusion that it is only the humanity of Christ that effects justification or redemption. Certainly such a doctrine would be deeply alien to Paul, who had virtually no interest in the humanity of Christ, but so likewise is it alien to every Christianity that knows redemption as the act of God and the act of God alone, or to every Christianity that knows predestination itself.

Yet thinking predestination is thinking that absolute No of God which is the absolute Yes of God. Here that No and that Yes are inseparable if not indistinguishable, as most manifest in every genuine thinking of the Crucifixion. If the Crucifixion realizes eternal life only by realizing eternal death, that eternal death is absolutely essential to this eternal life, so that here to think eternal life or redemption is to think eternal death or damnation. Barth understood this profoundly, but so, too, did Hegel, Kierkegaard, and Nietzsche, and here lies a clear dividing line between a truly modern and all premodern Western thinking, one most concretely manifest in the very movement of eternal return, an eternal return which all premodern thinking knows as the very movement of redemption itself, and an eternal return which is shattered in the very advent of the modern world. Initially, this shattering is most openly manifest in a negation of immortality, for with the closure of the backward movement of eternal return there can be no return to an original or primordial condition of immortality. Hence immortality becomes ever more deeply manifest as an illusion, and as a pathological illusion turning us away from the actuality of life and the world. Only then could theologians identify immortality as a truly pagan belief, one the very opposite of faith in the resurrection, and only then could theologians identify faith itself as an eschatological faith, one directed to an absolute future rather than an absolute or primordial past.

Yet once the movement of eternal return is profoundly challenged, this brings a wholly new meaning to genesis itself. Now genesis cannot be an absolute beginning whose end is absolute beginning itself. Every ultimate identity of Alpha and Omega is now ended, and therefore Godhead itself can no longer be known as an eternal movement of eternal return. Ever more gradually I became awakened to the necessity of understanding the genesis of God, and not a genesis of God which is an eternal genesis of God, but far rather a genesis of God which is a once and for all genesis of God, one which as such can never be repeated or renewed, and one whose inevitable destiny is the death of God. Now it becomes overwhelmingly important to understand an eternal death of God which is not the eternal resurrection of God, a death of God finally shattering every possible movement of eternal return, and a death of God absolutely necessary to apocalypse itself, and an apocalypse wholly and totally transcending genesis itself. Only now did it fully become clear to me that if the death of God has actually occurred then the very actuality of this death is inseparable from the genesis of God. For only that which has actually begun can actually die, and if God has truly and actually died then God Himself is inevitably the consequence of a truly actual genesis or beginning. Thereby I was given my most original theological idea, for even if it is deeply grounded in both Blake and Hegel, so far as I know it had never been given a fully explicit or systematic theological formulation.

One of the deep challenges I faced in late middle age was the probability that my thinking would become ever more fully unoriginal and ever more deeply conservative. This is a virtually universal phenomenon in the worlds that I have known, and it is surely true throughout the world of modern theology. It is clearest in both Barth and Tillich. The third volume of Tillich's *Systematic Theology* is not only truly conservative but derivative and unoriginal as well; and we see this movement occurring far more fully and decisively in Barth's *Church Dogmatics*, as all the power of its first two volumes appears to ever more fully and decisively reverse itself in its third and fourth volumes. Even Bultmann illustrates the apparently demonic consequences of aging, and in his final publication, a commentary on Second Corinthians, he goes so far as virtually to eliminate the Pauline ground of his *Theology of the New Testament* by arguing that for Paul God only regarded Christ as a sinner, as opposed to his earlier position that God made Christ to be sin so that we might become righteous. Of course, Augustine did his deepest theological thinking in his final years, but Augustine is far too distant from me to be a possible model at this point, and as I observed the contemporary world of theology, all of my fears were only deepened. So even if the very idea of a unique and once and for all genesis of God is a deeply demonic if not Satanic theological idea, I opened myself to it as a gift of grace, and could assure myself that I was not yet dead theologically.

I realized at once that this very idea brings a truly new meaning to the absolute Yes and the absolute No of God, one making possible a realization that it is only the genesis of God which makes possible a deep dichotomy between the affirmative and the negative poles of the Godhead, so that creation is not only fall, but as Blake knew so deeply, it is the fall of Godhead itself. Yet finally this ultimate fall is a fortunate fall, for it and it alone makes possible apocalypse itself. While such thinking is potentially if not actually present in *The Self-Embodiment of God* and *History as Apocalypse*, it is first systematically expressed in *Genesis and Apocalypse* and *The Genesis of God*, and if nothing else the writing of these books assured me that I was certainly not moving in a conservative theological direction. The non-theologian cannot realize how solitary this movement is in our theological world, or our manifest if not our true theological world, and now I was coming to know a solitude far deeper than I had previously known, just as I became ever more fully possessed by an interior necessity to retire from the academic world. Long before this I knew the necessity of solitude for genuine theological work. This had been my primary motive in seeking a monastic vocation. I have always thought that a monastic vocation is more conducive to theology than an academic vocation, so that I looked upon my academic vocation itself as a decisive sign of failure, and this only deepened as I ever more fully experienced the contemporary university world.

One of the lessons that I learned in the English department at Stony Brook is the truly negative effect which academic life has upon our poets. I came to rejoice that Blake had not had a single day of formal education, and I struggled to find a nonacademic theological style; this partially occurred in my early decision to renounce documentation, but it was most demanded in theological language itself, which I became ever more fully persuaded had become poisoned by its academic robes. Here, too, one can deeply venerate a Kierkegaard or a Nietzsche or a Wittgenstein, just as one can long for an edition of the *Summa Theologica* which would strip it of its scholastic setting, or a scholarly journal free of all scholarly authority. The very question of authority is deeply important here, raising the question of what could be a genuine theological authority; as everyone knows the Devil can quote scripture, and the theologian knows this more deeply than anyone else, just as the theologian knows that there can be a truly demonic theology, and if it is my theology which in our world has most commonly evoked this identification, I came to see this as a positive theological sign. Is it truly possible theologically to think the death of God, and, if so, is not this very thinking a theological warrant for thinking the genesis of God? For I became deeply persuaded that it is not possible to think the death of God without thinking the genesis of God, and this can only mean that it is not possible to think the crucifixion of God without thinking the genesis of God.

Sacrifice had long been a primal motif of my religious or theological thinking. I had long believed that sacrifice is the deepest and the purest movement of religion, and I had known that there are profound religious traditions which center upon sacrifice as the original moment or movement of creation. And if the sacrifice of God is the center of Christian redemption, could not the sacrifice of the Godhead be the center of the creation or of genesis itself? Creation is commonly known by the theologian as an act of absolute power, but there are deep traditions which know creation as a purely kenotic act of absolute self-emptying, and this does make possible for the theologian an understanding of how God the Creator could be the Crucified God, and of how the absolute sovereignty of God could be inseparable from the absolute sacrifice of God in Christ. Thereby God the Creator and God the Redeemer could truly be known as one God, and the death of God could truly be known as the death of *God*. Insofar as the Creator is known as an absolutely transcendent and absolutely sovereign Creator there can be no possibility of the Creator being known as the Crucified God, nor an actual possibility of knowing God the Creator as God the Redeemer, or not insofar as redemption occurs through the Crucifixion, or through the sacrifice of God. But insofar as creation itself can be known as sacrifice, and as an absolute sacrifice, then God the Redeemer can be known as God the Creator, and the Godhead of Christ be known as Godhead itself.

This has always been extraordinarily difficult in Christian theology, hence Arianism has long been the deepest Christian heresy, and the mother of all heresies, but Christian orthodoxy itself can be identified as Arian insofar as it refuses the Crucified God as God, or insofar as it refuses the sacrifice of Christ as the sacrifice of God. While it is true that neither the image nor the idea of the Crucified God are born until the full advent of modernity, modern theologians beginning with Luther can know the Crucified God, and know the Crucified God as deeply Pauline theologians. For if God was in Christ reconciling the world to Himself, and doing so solely through the death of Christ, then how could the crucified Lord not be God Himself? True, this could only be an absolute offense, but the Crucifixion itself is an absolute offense, and is called forth as such by Paul himself, and an offense not only to reason but also to faith, or to every faith not deeply and ultimately grounded in the Crucifixion. Genuine offense is an offense to theological thinking itself, so to think theologically in this sense is to assault oneself, and this could only be a deep assault upon every interior depth to which one is open, and therefore an assault upon everything which we can apprehend as God. Only such an assault can make possible the depths of offense, so that here theological thinking is inevitably a purely negative thinking, and finally it can think only by assaulting Godhead itself.

And what could be a greater assault upon Godhead itself than thinking the genesis of God? This is a far graver assault than any possible atheism, or any possible pure atheism; for it thinks not so as to dissolve the Godhead, but far rather to reverse Godhead itself, and to reverse the eternity of Godhead itself, an eternity inseparable from everything that we have apprehended or known as the Godhead. The opening chapters of *Genesis and Apocalypse* most deeply intend to reverse the primordial movement of eternal return, a movement which has been an ultimate ground of everything that we have known as the Godhead, and a movement which is here understood to have been absolutely reversed by genesis or absolute beginning, an absolute beginning which is the absolute ending of eternal return, and therefore the ending of every possible primordial eternity. More concretely, this is an attempt to reverse everything that Eliade understands as eternal return, and everything that Hegel understands as eternity itself; for even if Hegel could profoundly reverse that "Bad Infinite" which is the very opposite of the finite, he could never reverse eternity itself, and therefore could only finally know the crucifixion of God as the resurrection of God. No, if the death of God is an ultimate and final event, then eternity itself is shattered, and that shattering most deeply occurs at the center of Godhead itself, and at the center of that Godhead which is known or manifest as an eternal movement of eternal return.

Both *Genesis and Apocalypse* and *The Genesis of God* attempt to understand a primordial totality or a primordial eternity as that very totality which is ultimately and finally shattered and reversed by the absolute act of genesis itself. Therefore it is primordial totality itself which is shattered by the Creator, a primordial totality which is primordial Godhead, so that the Godhead of the Creator is a reversal of the primordial Godhead. How is it possible to think this? First, and perhaps most important, is the necessity of establishing a real and actual distinction between God and the Godhead, or between the Creator and a primordial totality, with the consequent necessity of understanding how the Creator evolves out of the Godhead. Ancient Neoplatonism could do this in its understanding of the emanation of the Godhead, an understanding deeply paralleled in both Hindu and Buddhist philosophy, and one which is seemingly resurrected or renewed in the deeper or more mystical expressions of Christian Neoplatonism. But all of this thinking is a thinking of eternal return, as most openly manifest in its ultimate identification of Alpha and Omega, or of an absolute beginning and an absolute ending. Even Hegel succumbs to this thinking in the *Science of Logic*, and if this is a deeply circular thinking which is a cyclical thinking, it finally thinks eternal return and eternal return alone, or does so apart from its most subversive sections.

Is there no way to establish a real distinction between God and the Godhead without thinking eternal return, or could there be any genuinely theological thinking which is not the thinking of eternal return, and not the thinking of the eternal return of that Godhead which is primordial totality itself? Here it becomes overwhelmingly important to understand genesis or absolute beginning as a once and for all event, an understanding absent in every genuine thinking of eternal return, so that not only is it absent from the *Science of Logic*, but it is also absent from every non-Christian or non-Jewish or non-Islamic thinking, and every thinking truly independent of the Bible. Yet if the thinking of eternal return is a profoundly non-biblical thinking, how did it so fully enter Christian theology? Is this the inevitable consequence of the advent of philosophical theology, and hence the necessary consequence of pure thinking itself? Or is it the inevitable consequence of thinking pure transcendence itself, one which occurs only after the advent of Christianity. It is certainly absent in all pre-Christian philosophical thinking, and at no other point did Plotinus so deeply differ from Plato. Indeed, an actual thinking of eternal return does not occur in the West until the beginning of the Christian era, so that one might justly think that it does not and cannot occur in the West apart from the Christian God, although here the Christian God deeply differs from the biblical God, or from that biblical God who is the Creator.

Hence an assault upon eternal return could be understood as a witness to the biblical God, and here that assault must occur most fully within theology itself, and within every theology that is a theology of eternal return, or every theology ultimately and finally bound to a primordial eternity. Of course, this includes virtually every theology upon our horizon, and every theology thinking what we have most deeply been given as Godhead itself, an absolutely eternal and an absolutely transcendent Godhead, and one whose only movement is the movement of eternal return. Already Luther could know every "reason" as purely idolatrous, as an absolute rebellion against revelation, and Luther was not philosophically ignorant. He had been deeply trained in that "new philosophy" of Occamism, a philosophy truly knowing the absolute transcendence of God. Is it that absolute transcendence itself which is our purest "idol," and could it be said that it could only truly be manifest or real as a consequence of an ultimate and final fall, a fall wherein Godhead itself can only be known as absolute transcendence? Such a pure and radical transcendence is wholly opposed to that total presence which is the presence of primordial Godhead, just as it is wholly opposed to the total presence of apocalyptic Godhead or Omega. Thus the pure transcendence of God is truly other than Godhead itself, and if this transcendence itself is the consequence of an ultimate fall, that could only be a fall from primordial Godhead, or a fall dividing and dichotomizing Godhead itself. And if such a fall could be understood as a once and for all fall, or an absolutely unique as opposed to an absolutely eternal fall, or as that fall which is the absolute act of absolute beginning, then that beginning could not be an eternal beginning, just as its ending could not be only a repetition of absolute beginning. For this fall could occur only by way of an absolute disruption of eternal return, and therefore an absolute reversal of the eternal return of Godhead itself.

Is it possible to realize a theology that is a true disruption or reversal of eternal return, a theology genuinely reversing the eternal return of the Godhead, and thereby reversing eternal return itself? Nietzsche is a supreme challenge here. Is his vision of eternal recurrence a resurrection or renewal of the primordial vision of eternal return, or is it the very opposite of every movement of eternal return, and opposite insofar as it is a forward rather than a backward movement to eternity? I ever more fully came to understand that Nietzsche's revolutionary thinking of eternal recurrence embodies our most ultimate unthinking of eternal return, and does so most clearly in its inseparability from Nietzsche's proclamation of the death of God. Here only the death of God makes possible an enactment of eternal recurrence, an enactment which is an absolute Yes-saying to an absolute immanence, and an absolute immanence which is the consequence of the death of God. No thinker has more deeply unthought an absolute transcendence than did Nietzsche, and this most deeply occurs in the thinking of eternal recurrence, an eternal recurrence absolutely ending all transcendence, and doing so by reversing every backward movement to eternity, or by reversing every movement of eternal return. Yet Nietzsche's vision of eternal recurrence can also be understood as a uniquely modern enactment of predestination, as I attempt to do in the chapter on Nietzsche in *Gen-*

esis and Apocalypse. Here, too, we find an ultimate enactment of an absolute Yes-saying which is an absolute No-saying, and one which is not only absolutely necessary, but now absolutely inescapable for everyone as a consequence of the death of God. No thinker has understood the Crucifixion so purely as did Nietzsche, and no other thinker has so purely understood predestination itself, a predestination which is not only an absolute necessity, but it only fully or truly becomes manifest as that necessity with the uniquely modern realization of the death of God, a death of God hurling us into a new and absolute nothingness, yet that nothingness is the very arena of that predestination which is eternal recurrence. Nietzsche, too, deeply understood the genesis of God, although he never spoke of it as such. He rather knew that genesis as an ultimate genealogy, a genealogy revolving about the advent of No-saying or the "bad conscience," an advent which is the advent of interiority itself, an interiority whose only real movement is *ressentiment*, and a *ressentiment* only made possible by an absolute No-saying, which is Nietzsche's deepest name of the uniquely Christian God.

So that here the Christian God is wholly inseparable from an original and absolute fall, a fall which is the advent not only of history but of a purely negative interiority, and no thinker has known an original fall more deeply or more comprehensively than did Nietzsche. Theologically, that fall could only be the fall of Godhead itself, and while Nietzsche did not actually say this, his very language about God—and Nietzsche speaks of God more fully than any other philosopher except for Spinoza and Hegel—is a purely negative language, one calling forth only an absolutely lacerating or absolutely negative power. Only Joyce rivals, if he does not surpass, Nietzsche's blasphemy, and just as Joyce enacted an eternal return in his epics, this return is not a backward movement to eternity, but rather a forward movement to an absolute chaos, an absolute chaos which is apocalypse itself, so that here, too, we discover the forward movement of eternal recurrence rather than the backward movement of eternal return. Both in Joyce and Nietzsche, eternal recurrence is a purely and ultimately apocalyptic movement, one finally ending every possible transcendence, and one finally realizing a truly new world or new creation, but only insofar as the old creation comes to an end, or only insofar as the original Creator is dead. Yet that Creator could truly die only if that Creator has truly begun, and if it is truly possible to apprehend an absolute beginning, then that absolute beginning must truly transcend eternity itself, or truly transcend a primordial eternity or a primordial totality, a transcendence which it is possible to know as the genesis of God.

Or is that an actual possibility, and an actual possibility for theology itself? Even if this would be an understanding of God the Creator as the Crucified God, and hence an understanding finally knowing crucifixion and creation as one act, how is it possible to understand an ultimate identity between creation and crucifixion? First, this could be possible because it understands the act of creation as an absolutely self-negating or self-emptying act, an act wherein and whereby a primordial eternity or totality absolutely negates itself, and only this self-negation truly ends that totality. But this is an ending reversing that totality, and one giving birth to absolute transcendence itself. Second, this also could be possible if it makes possible an understanding of absolute act itself, an act absolutely transforming everything whatsoever, and therefore an act which is absolutely new, and whose very absolute newness is an absolute reversal of eternal return, an eternal return foreclosing every possibility of the actually or truly new. Third, only an understanding of the genesis of God makes possible an actual understanding of the death of God, so that to accept the death of God in the Crucifixion as the true center of faith is to accept the necessity of understanding the genesis of God, and the death of that Creator who is destined or predestined to eternal death. Finally, only an understanding of the genesis of God makes possible a truly or fully apocalyptic theology, one knowing the absolute future as the absolute ending of every past, and above all of every past which can be known or apprehended as a primordial past, or of that past which is the primordial movement of eternal return.

While these are all powerful motifs for me, I must confess that I have had little success in communicating them to others. This has often led me to the verge of despair, but I have not been suicidal in my later years, not even tempted by suicide, I must confess, which sometimes makes me wonder if I am truly serious. I have a genuine confidence in the solidity and the responsibility of my theological vision, and while I am deeply critical of most of my executions of that vision, and often think that impatience is my worst fault, I fully confess that I think that excess is far preferable to reticence, or is so for me, and this largely because we have been thrust into such a deep theological void. I am sometimes asked why I do not couch my theological language in the form of thought-experiments, or even in the form of a Wittgensteinian game, but I doubt if my Calvinism would allow this, and that very Kierkegaard who wrote of thought-experiments never actually employed such language in his own real thinking, even if he could effectively employ it in his assaults upon Hegel. No, Stonewall remains my deep ancestor, and I, too, am called to battle, and even a murderous battle, for I most deeply know the true theologian as the murderer of God.

CHAPTER 11

Prayer

David Jasper, an Anglican theologian who is a major figure in the field of literature and theology, and a genuine and original theologian in his own right, affirms in his review of my book *The Contemporary Jesus*, that this book is truly literature and theology at the very cutting edge of thought and, dare one say, "prayer." This response came as a real surprise to me, and it had never occurred before; indeed, I am unaware of any contemporary theological book being associated with prayer, and this, too, is a deep distinction between pre-contemporary and contemporary theology. Theology had once been thought of as a form of prayer, just as deep thinking itself had been so identified, and while this has occurred in our world only in Heidegger and Levinas, it is perhaps most absent in theology itself, where prayer itself has become an ultimate mystery. This is a mystery that had long summoned me, and just as the death of God controversy erupted I had been involved in a project to prepare a text on the contemporary reality of prayer, a text issuing from reflections on prayer by Trappist monks in their monastery in Conyers, Georgia. Claude McCaleb had been responsible for this project. He was an editor and publisher at Bobbs-Merrill who later married my sister, Jane, and he was responsible for Bobbs-Merrill becoming for a brief period the major publisher of radical theological books. They had also sponsored two conferences on the death of God theology, and we even attempted to establish a radical theology journal, but this floundered when I could only procure enough articles for one issue (my first disillusionment with fellow radical theologians). I had taken Claude to the monastery, and when he learned that many of the monks there thought very little of contemporary books on prayer, he induced them to initiate a project that would rectify this grave deficiency.

The idea was that a group of about half a dozen of the monks would meet weekly to discuss the actual meaning and praxis of prayer today. I would be there to do no more than act as a moderator. The sessions would be recorded, and then later we would edit these for publication. Let me say at once that I had a deep rapport with these monks, truly respecting them, and, yes, respecting them theologically. Nowhere else have I encountered a community so deeply Christian and so deeply radical at once; and their project was more radical then mine, I never doubted this, and I still do not doubt that nothing is more needed today than a genuine theology of prayer. They were determined to end every distinction between the sacred and the profane or the heavenly and the earthly in the understanding and practice of prayer, to draw forth prayer as an enactment of life itself, and more specifically to understand Christian prayer as a profoundly incarnational prayer, one realized in the depths of life and the world itself, and one whose occurrence is a universal occurrence in full actuality or full life itself. To cite but one example, the only contemporary book on prayer that they could take seriously was Teilhard's *The Divine Milieu*. Now this is remarkable not only because Trappists could think highly of a Jesuit book on prayer, but because this is a book that so frequently is deeply condemned in orthodox Catholic circles. Of course, I had long known that contemplative monks are deeply independent of the Catholic hierarchy, but I encountered here a genuine freedom in the monastic life which I have never encountered in secular life, and certainly never encountered in the university world.

Unfortunately this project was never completed; perhaps it was far more difficult than we initially realized. Indeed, I suspect that nothing is more difficult today than understanding prayer theologically, nor do we have a genuine understanding of prayer from any perspective whatsoever. There are many times when I believe that the foremost theological challenge today is an understanding of prayer, although this may finally be simply impossible. One of the most intriguing theological challenges of our new world is the great popularity of liturgical and meditative music; perhaps only here is genuine music responded to in "postmodernity," only here that depth in music can be heard universally, or only here that depth in our world is manifest at all. It is true that music is universal in the world of religion, and can retain its power even when the mythical or doctrinal expressions of religion are in abeyance; this is most striking if not most paradoxical in our new world, when theology has either disappeared or become wholly frozen, and yet a genuinely sacred music exercises deep power, and apparently far more so than any other form of music, or any other form of art. Is ours a world in which only the purest forms of the sacred can induce an ultimate response? And is this accompanied by a genuine if not ultimate dissolution of every other form of the sacred, thus bringing a crisis not only to every institutional expression of religion, but to every expression of our culture itself?

Music is our only art in which the sacred is truly universal, and so much so that it is extraordinarily difficult to discover a genuine music which is genuinely profane. Perhaps if only for this reason even in the twentieth century our major composers are more deeply religious as a body than any other body of artists; and if the musical performer is more truly disciplined than any other artist in our world, this could be understood not only as an ultimate but as a sacred discipline, and truly sacred in its very ultimacy. Although my own theological work is most deeply dependent upon Christian epic poetry, it has always been inspired by music, and I have long given fuller attention to music than to any other art, hearing in music a power that I could apprehend as a theological power, and ultimately a power that is the power of prayer itself, so that if only here even we are given a genuine language of prayer. Is it possible to translate that power into an open theological language? I believe that this has occurred again and again in our purer literary works, and while I know full well that I am incapable of writing such a work, I did attempt a novel that was given to this goal. Entitled "Laura: A Portrait of a Contemporary Saint," the project was much affected by Leon Bloy's judgment that there is but one sorrow and that is not to be a saint, but far more affected by the goal of attempting to discover a contemporary language of prayer.

One of the major accomplishments of literary scholarship in our world is our truly new biographies of our great novelists, wherein it is demonstrated how fully our novelists have incorporated their own lives into their novels; and while I would never compare myself to such novelists, it is true that my novel revolves about an ultimate initiation of Laura's that parallels my own initiation into Satan, and that here only a voyage into the depths of darkness makes possible a genuine language of prayer. Perhaps I was attempting to discover in Laura what I cannot discover in myself, a truly shamanic initiation, one releasing the purest light out of the purest darkness, a light which is a genuinely embodied light, and one only possible by way of a pure embodiment of pure darkness itself. Of course, I was deeply influenced by Dostoyevsky, and by Bernanos, too, in whom we once again encounter the deeply Christian motif of the Descent into Hell, and I had become persuaded that a genuine Christian sanctity is possible only by way of such a descent. Although it is true that this is a universal movement in the Christian epic, it is virtually absent from Christian theology, which itself could be a reason why our modern Christian theology cannot be a theology of prayer.

It is difficult for me to understand how I could ever have thought that I was capable of writing a novel. I certainly lack all the powers demanded of a novelist, all perhaps save a certain kind of introspection, an introspection seeking the deepest moment of one's life, and attempting to unfold that moment as a liberating moment, and a liberation most deeply from oneself. This was the intended core of this very mediocre novel, but the challenge that overwhelmed me as the greatest challenge was writing Laura's internal reflections, and above all her reflections upon that initiation which had occurred in a suddenly discovered clearing in a dark wood. Then she was immediately hurled into a center of darkness, and a center which she thereafter knew as ultimate center itself. I attempt to call forth that center as a primal source of ultimate power for Laura herself, and while I fail to capture it in Laura's own language, I would like to think that it is at least evoked in the reactions of others to Laura, and perhaps abstractly called forth in Laura's reflections upon Spinoza's God. Many of my literary colleagues were persuaded that it is impossible for the novel to be philosophical or theoretical, but I think that this is true only of the English or of the contemporary novel, and while I could only write a novel that is against the grain, I think that every great novel is finally theological, and most theological in its purest language, a language finally evoking God.

But is it possible for our language about God to be a language of prayer? Perhaps this is true only in literature, and in our deepest literature, so this all too mediocre novel of mine might be thought of as a writing-experiment, an experiment to see if it is possible for the theologian to employ the genre of the novel in seeking a language of prayer, with the presumption that a language of prayer is impossible in our contemporary theological languages. Here, we must accept the truth that prayer is inevitably a deep mystery to us, a mystery that we might approach by acknowledging that genuine prayer will inevitably be truly other than everything that is manifest or namable as prayer to us, and that it might well most be real where we least expect it, and where it is most unnamable as prayer. I could not say that I have known more than a few who could practice anything that I could know as prayer, but then I believe that we all pray in our most unguarded moments, or our moments when we are least ourselves; and just as I have never been able to abandon prayer, I find it very difficult to believe that this is possible for anyone, just as I cannot believe that ultimate barriers between us can be released apart from prayer. Now even if this is true, is an actual language of prayer possible for us, and a language in genuine continuity with our traditional language of prayer, or a language in continuity with our liturgical and meditative language?

Once I entered into community with a group of California Congregationalist pastors seeking a new Christian life; they implored me to write a creed for their project. I foolishly accepted, and at the publisher's request it was included as an appendix to *The Genesis of God*. This is not only an apocalyptic creed, but a creed which I intended as an apocalyptic prayer, and a prayer which I trust can be heard in an actual reading of the creed:

> I believe in the triumph of the Kingdom of God, in that Kingdom which is the final life of the spirit, a life incarnate in Jesus, and consummated in his death. That death is the self-embodiment of the Kingdom of God, and a death which is the resurrection of incarnate body, a body which is a glorified body, but glorified only in its crucifixion, which is the death of all heavenly spirit, and the life of a joy which is grace incarnate. That joy and grace are all in all, offered everywhere and to everyone, and invisible and unreal only to these who refuse them, a refusal which is everyone's but a refusal which is annulled in the death of the incarnate and crucified God, and transfigured in that resurrection, a resurrection which is the actual and present glory of the Kingdom of God. Amen.

If nothing else I hope that this creed makes manifest how far the Apostles Creed is from apocalyptic Christianity, but it is also intended to make clear that a genuine creed is a genuine prayer, so that a genuine language of belief is a language of prayer, and when creed loses that ground it truly becomes heteronomous or demonic.

My youngest sister Nell is the one in our family most like myself. She became a genuine poet, and moved from Catholicism to a genuinely religious form of atheism, and yet there is a true consistency in this move, as her mature poetry is clearly a poetry of prayer, and while possessed by a genuine rage, which in its radical feminist form was often directed at me, she simply cannot escape a language of prayer in her own deeper poetry. I sense that this is true of every genuine poet, and finally true of us all, and yet nothing is more difficult today than the actual language of prayer. We all know the deeply disruptive consequences of the Catholic Church's adoption of a vernacular liturgy, with apparently no prior awareness of the extraordinary difficulty of translating a liturgical language into a vernacular language, and above all so in our world. W. H. Auden once remarked to me that he resigned from the commission preparing a revision of the *Book of Common Prayer* because he was alone in that body in being determined to preserve a sacred language of prayer, and alone because he was the only poet in that group, the only one with a sense of sacred language itself.

This is a genuine problem in our world and it is dramatically manifest in late modern or contemporary translations of the Bible, and while it is true that most biblical scholars have little sense of the sacrality of language, and are trained in such a way as to dilute or dissolve any such sensibility, the deeper problem is the chasm between our contemporary languages and the languages of those worlds which gave us our classical translations of the Bible. In this perspective, we can see that the death of God is embodied in our language itself, and hence inevitably embodied in contemporary vernacular liturgies or contemporary translations of the Bible. At one time I was deeply affected by the liturgical movement in the Catholic Church, much caught up in its determination to transform a medieval hierarchical liturgy into a truly communal liturgy, one inspired by its demonstration of the profound transformation of the liturgy which had occurred in its medieval development, with a consequent call of return to a pre-Constantinian liturgy, and even a return to a primitive Christian liturgy. Unfortunately, that liturgy is truly apocalyptic, thus seemingly wholly alien to our world, unless our world is finally an apocalyptic world, and hence one open to a truly apocalyptic prayer.

The liturgical scholar who most affected me was the Anglican Benedictine monk Dom Gregory Dix, whom I once consulted about my own possible monastic vocation. His book *The Shape of the Liturgy* had a fundamental impact upon me, and particularly so its crucial section on the most important of all the words in the Christian liturgy, *anamnesis*: "Do this in *anamnesis* of me" (I Corinthians 11:25). While commonly translated as "memory" or "remembrance," Dix insists that *anamnsesis* here must be understood as re-presentation or renewal, not an interior memory, but far rather an actual calling forth of the Crucifixion itself, a liturgical enactment and renewal of the one source of redemption. This is the real work or action of the liturgy, and in participating in the liturgy we actually participate in that re-presentation or renewal. Although Dix minimizes the apocalyptic ground of the liturgy, this is overwhelmingly clear in Paul's account of the institution of the Eucharist: "for as often as you eat this bread and drink the cup, you proclaim the Lord's death until he comes" (I Corinthians 11:26). Certainly the Eucharist which Paul celebrates is an apocalyptic Eucharist, and one could surmise that the very absence of the Eucharist from the Fourth Gospel is the absence of an apocalyptic enactment, just as its centrality in the Book of Revelation is the centrality of an apocalyptic enactment.

Again and again I have been deeply affected by Kierkegaard's insistence that the deepest difference between biblical faith and paganism is that the latter is grounded in remembrance and the former in repetition, the one in a backward movement of return and the other in a forward movement of repetition; and this deep insight certainly illuminates both apocalyptic prayer and an apocalyptic liturgy. Here prayer and liturgy are not a backward movement of remembrance or memorial, but rather a forward movement, and a forward movement finally directed to apocalypse itself. Yet this is the very movement which is most fully transformed both in the ancient Christian liturgy and in ancient Christian prayer, as a backward movement of eternal return ever increasingly dominates the liturgy and the prayer of the Church, and a primitive Christian prayer and liturgy all but disappears. Why is this of so little interest to the historian of Christianity or to the theological world itself? Have we lost all sense of apocalyptic prayer, or simply all sense of prayer itself? I believe that at no other point is the death of God more fully manifest in our world, and yet apparently only a death of God theologian can see this. Is this because it is only in understanding the death of God that we can understand the depth and ultimacy of our actual condition?

There is substantial critical agreement that Barth's fundamental transformation of his own work proceeded from his discovery of and book on Anselm, that Anselm who is the Western theologian above all others for whom theology itself is prayer, and we can discover a progressive diminution if not reversal of this identification in the subsequent development of Western theology. At no other point is there a more ultimate chasm between Eastern and Western theology, so that Western Christians have inevitably been drawn to Eastern Christianity at this crucial point, and even if Byzantine theology is truly alien to the West, Russian Christianity has had a deep impact upon the West in late modernity. I must confess that I most purely discovered the death of God in Dostoyevsky's *The Possessed* or *Demons*, and here the purest language of the death of God is a language of prayer. Kirillov is clearly both an atheistic and an apocalyptic saint, and this is a pure atheism that is a pure apocalypticism, so that Kirillov lives and dies an apocalypse that is an atheistic apocalypse, and yet an atheistic apocalypse that is an *anamnesis* of Jesus himself. Theologically, what is most remarkable about Kirillov's language is that it is so manifestly a language of prayer. This can even be observed in its agrammatical structure, a language that must distance itself from all established grammar; only that dissonance here makes possible a language of prayer, and a truly apocalyptic language of prayer. Is this a language evoking the death of God as the ultimate apocalyptic event?

Upon reflection I gradually came to realize that the truest language of the death of God is a language of prayer. I have come to think that this is finally true even of Hegel, and in the *Phenomenology of Spirit* the purest enactments of the death of God are explicitly enactments of kenosis. This, too, can be understood as an *anamnesis* of the Crucifixion, and if here pure thinking is an ultimate thinking of self-negation or self-emptying, such self-emptying can be understood as prayer itself, and as a genuinely apocalyptic prayer. Of course, this movement is fully explicit and undeniable in Blake's mature work, but could this possibly be true in Nietzsche's proclamation of the death of God? Can we understand the language of this "Madman" as a language of prayer? Certainly this is an apocalyptic language, must it therefore of necessity be a language of prayer? Is it possible to enact apocalypse itself apart from apocalyptic prayer, or apart from a language renewing or reenacting Jesus's eschatological proclamation and enactment of the Kingdom of God? Nietzsche's is the first philosophical language to be a fully explicit apocalyptic language. Is that possible apart from apocalyptic prayer, or apart from an apocalyptic *anamnesis* of the Crucifixion itself?

The very word *anamnesis* became overwhelming for me, and just as I could see how its original Christian enactment had been truly transformed in the prayer and the liturgy of the church, I became ever more open to the possibility that it had truly been reborn in a uniquely modern atheism, and most clearly so in the apocalyptic enactments of that atheism. But how can such enactments be understood as enactments of prayer? If there is a truly unique Christian expression of prayer, and if this is enacted in the earliest Christian liturgy, could this enactment be a truly apocalyptic enactment, and one which undergoes a genuine *anamnesis* in every subsequent apocalyptic enactment, and even does so in a seemingly atheistic enactment? Certainly one deep and ultimate enactment is shared by ancient and modern apocalypticism, and that is an absolute Yes-saying, an absolute celebration of the deepest possible Yes, one occurring in response to the Crucifixion itself, and thus in response to the death of God. Paul's eucharistic language calls forth this death more decisively than does his purely theological language, and if we proclaim the "Lord's death" as often as we eat this bread and drink this cup, is that not the truest possible liturgical action, and the deepest possible liturgical prayer? But is that a liturgical action and prayer which can be understood as becoming universalized with the uniquely modern realization of the death of God?

Is it possible truly to say Yes to the death of God apart from prayer, or is Yes-saying itself possible apart from the deepest prayer, and is this a Yes-saying first corporately enacted in the Eucharist itself? D. G. Leahy is the only thinker whom I know who has actually and fully attempted to think the Eucharist, and if this entails a transformation of the *missa solemnis* into the *missa jubilaea*, this is a truly apocalyptic transformation, and one which can be understood to be in

genuine continuity with the original Eucharist. True, Leahy can understand my theology as an inversion and reversal of the eucharistic substance to the form of the dark identity of the immediate actuality of
experience, an inversion and reversal which is a Black Mass (*Foundation*, page 536), an abysmal theology which also can be characterized
as a "non-Eucharistic Eucharistic externality" (page 468). Leahy's
understanding of Matter or the Body itself is simultaneously an apocalyptic and a liturgical understanding; here totality itself is a eucharistic
Body, but a eucharistic Body only insofar as it is an apocalyptic Body,
and a eucharistic Body which is the transformation of God as God,
hence a eucharistic Body which is the apocalyptic resurrection of God.

Now if this is the first time that a eucharistic language has fully
been employed as a language about God, this may well be the advent
of a genuinely liturgical theology, one which has never occurred
before, and when it does occur it can only occur as a purely apocalyptic theology, and an apocalyptic theology enacting the cosmic and total
Yes of the *missa jubilaea*. Leahy's thinking is not only a pure and total
thinking, but it is a pure thinking which is pure prayer. Perhaps this is
a primal reason why Leahy's work is so comprehensively ignored in
our world, but it does fully demonstrate that pure thinking can be pure
prayer, and perhaps inevitably so in a genuinely apocalyptic thinking.
Why should we think that Anselm's thinking is a genuine expression
of prayer whereas Hegel's thinking clearly is not, or that Augustine's
thinking is clearly a prayerful thinking and Nietzsche's thinking certainly is not? Is this because we simply cannot imagine a uniquely
modern expression of prayer? And also because we cannot imagine a
uniquely modern apocalypse? But this has certainly been given us, and
most clearly given us in a uniquely modern epic poetry, a poetry
which can be understood as prayer, and is even explicitly enacted as
prayer, and even as a fully liturgical prayer, as in *Finnegans Wake*.

The occasions in which I have had the fullest sense of communion
with an audience have been those in which I attempted oral readings
from *Finnegans Wake*. Then I did actually experience something of
what Leahy understands as the *missa jubilaea*, a truly cosmic mass,
but a cosmic mass which is an apocalyptic mass, and one being
enacted in our very midst. Everyone can seemingly be open to this
mass, for this is a truly universal mass, and I simply cannot imagine
how anyone could truly or finally resist it, or anyone who could hear

it, and even if it can only be heard as an ultimate chaos, here that chaos is an ecstatic Yes, and a Yes that is inevitably celebrated insofar as it is heard. An ultimate and final celebration is a decisive key to this mass, and if such a celebration has always been the truest center of the Eucharist, and one whose history goes back to the very advent of humanity itself, so that every genuine mass is a universal mass, the very presence of this celebration is a witness to the enactment of this mass. Here celebration itself is deep prayer, and a deep prayer inseparable from ecstatic joy. Clearly that joy can be evoked by oral readings of *Finnegans Wake*, then if only vicariously we participate in this mass, but if we actually and fully hear these words, that very hearing could only be a sacramental hearing, one inseparable from the brute actuality of these words.

Is an ecstatic joy possible for us? But that is also to ask if an apocalyptic prayer is possible for us, and here we must inevitably recall the closing words of the Christian Bible: "Amen. Come, Lord Jesus!" This is perhaps the purest of all apocalyptic prayers; it certainly was a center of the original Eucharist, and here we can understand that the "real presence" is an apocalyptic presence, and one not confined to the *missa solemnis*, but universally present in a *missa jubilaea*. Here is an ecstatic celebration which is the celebration of life and body itself, and a celebration of that universal body which is an apocalyptic body; so that to hear joy itself is to hear this body, and not to hear it in "heaven," but to hear it on "earth," or to hear it in the deepest immediacy of life itself. True joy may well be the deepest mystery in our midst, but that joy is the consequence of an ultimate and final Yes, and if apocalyptic prayer is a praying of that Yes, here is our deepest summons to prayer, and a prayer which we hear when we hear joy itself. Have I heard that prayer? Yes, and heard it even if only hearing it in others, and heard it in truly hearing others; then silence truly ends, and then we ourselves can only say Yes. That Yes truly is apocalyptic prayer, and an apocalyptic prayer which we pray in actually saying Yes, so that if we have ever said Yes, and fully and actually said it, then even we have known apocalyptic prayer.

CHAPTER 12

Absolute Abyss

There is no greater challenge to faith than the pervasive judgment that faith is a flight from life, an evasion of pain and suffering, a refusal of the burden and the anguish of the human condition, or a capitulation to that passivity which is the very reversal of freedom and responsibility. Certainly I have always known faith as an ultimate challenge, and an ultimate challenge inseparable from a profound conflict, one which could be understood as an ultimate conflict between a pure activity and a pure passivity, or between a genuine freedom and a fully actual impotence. Insofar as Stonewall Jackson has been a model for my life, I have thought of this conflict as war itself, a deeply interior and yet violent war, one finally allowing no hostages or slackers, and demanding a ruthless discipline, and yet a discipline allowing if not impelling truly innovative tactics and strategy, for here the odds are overwhelmingly against victory, and even the very meaning of victory is deeply in question. While ultimately faith is a gift of grace, humanly it is an ultimate struggle, and the absence of struggle can be understood as an absence of faith, but the struggle itself can only be a truly individual struggle. Hence this is a struggle transcending any possible guidelines or rules, and wholly inseparable from one's unique condition and situation. Even Catholicism can know and accept the autonomy of the individual conscience, but so, too, is there a deep autonomy of faith itself, and even if there is an extraordinary variety and multiplicity of faith or faiths, each is individually enacted, and is only genuine faith to the extent that it is individually enacted, an enactment which itself is inseparable from a genuine struggle.

Inevitably that struggle occurs in a unique and particular world, so that there is a struggle for faith that is unique to our world, and I ever increasingly became persuaded that this can best be understood by way of the category of absolute nothingness, one that was deeply called forth philosophically in the nineteenth century, and far more comprehensively called forth imaginatively in full and late modernity, and it is certainly possible to understand a late modern and postmodern history and society as having a genuine ground in such a nothingness. It is important to distinguish a literal from an absolute nothingness, or a simple from an ultimate nothingness. Just as evil could traditionally be understood as a literal or truly simple nothingness, no such understanding is actually possible in our world; hence we have become bereft of actual conceptions of evil, and if only thereby inevitably bereft of actual conceptions of the good, so that if only in this sense our world is truly beyond good and evil, a beyondness inseparable from the advent of what can be named as an absolute nothingness. That is a nothingness assaulting if not dissolving our deepest ground, and it is certainly an ultimate challenge to faith itself, and just as it has generated truly new fundamentalisms throughout the world, it embodies a unique arena for the struggle of faith, one now truly inescapable, and inescapable if only because of the advent of a new and comprehensive nihilism, a nihilism which is now and for the first time our deepest and most universal challenge.

I had been very much aware of this challenge throughout my theological work, and I discovered that in intimate conversations with theologians this topic commonly arises, often hearing the judgment that a particular theology is hollow or unreal because it fails to meet this challenge, and again and again sharing the agonizing possibility that perhaps none of us can do this, and cannot do it if only because we lack an ultimate courage. If only through my fellow theologians I became persuaded that such a courage is now a truly necessary theological discipline, and while I am alone in centering my work upon damnation and Satan, I certainly am not alone in centering theology upon an absolute nothingness, and just as Hell can be known as a primal symbol of absolute nothingness, damnation can be known as a deeply modern if not universal condition, and one that becomes truly meaningful to us all through the language and the imagery of an absolute nothingness. I suspect that a primary reason why my fellow theologians refuse to employ the language of damnation and Hell is because of their intention if only at this point of distancing themselves from all theological orthodoxies, but it is remarkable that in our century both orthodox theologians and orthodox evangelists have abandoned or are abandoning the language of Hell and damnation. Perhaps at no other point is television evangelism more distant from traditional evangelism, or Barth's dogmatics more distant from all traditional dogmatics. Yet in the time of the Holocaust why are we so silent about Hell?

Ever more gradually I came to venerate our great artists for their profound courage. This is perhaps clearest in the modern world, and I can see that the modern artists whom I most venerate clearly embody an ultimate courage. Here Kafka and Beckett are primary models. Both not only confronted but luminously recorded an absolute nothingness, and the pure clarity of their writing evokes an awesome clarity of absolute nothingness itself, an absolute nothingness which is absolutely meaningful and absolutely meaningless at once, and which can truly be entered only by way of the deepest courage. In America, Melville, Dickinson, Faulkner, and Stevens evoke a comparable awe. Here lies a courage far deeper than our theologians have known, and if only at this point we can see the absurdity of all theological apologetics, and thereby, too, the absurdity of all theological language claiming ultimate depth, as though this had ever been reached by any of our modern theological languages. Here, it is also possible to see how lacking in courage we theologians are, how our very theologies shield us from the possibility of genuine courage, inevitably making of theology itself a way of *ressentiment*, a way for those lacking the courage of facing our actuality itself. The secular mind almost invariably knows theology as a way for the weak, and even if this is also true of our behaviorisms and our positivisms, and perhaps of every ideology whatsoever, it is uniquely damning for the theologian, and damning for the theologian if only because of the audacity of theology, for only theological language now claims to speak of God.

Just as the very word "God" has virtually disappeared from contemporary philosophical and literary language, it is now threatening to disappear from contemporary critical theological language. This is no doubt an extraordinary if not a unique condition, and it impels one to ask why this might be so. Here, our literary language is decisively important, and above all that late modern literary language which most seemingly evokes or names God, and while this never directly or openly occurs in our deeper literary language, just as it does not occur in a fully modern painting, here a theological naming is nevertheless overwhelmingly real, as I discovered in my studies of Joyce. But it is Kafka's naming of God which most deeply affected me, for this is surely the naming of an absolute darkness or an absolute nothingness. Kafka was an explorer in the truest possible sense, and one whose profound courage is unquestionable. Courage here is a deeply solitary courage, and I became persuaded that this, indeed, is a genuine theological model, and a model most clearly for the truly contemporary theologian, or for any contemporary quest for the meaning of God for us. Immediately we must note the deep difference between this way and all traditional negative theologies, for this way certainly does not lead to a dissolution of all ideas and images of God, but rather to their very reversal, a reversal leading not to an absolute darkness or absolute chaos that is a human or fallen reflection of the Godhead, but far rather to an absolute darkness that is Godhead itself.

It is with Ray Hart that I most deeply share this way, and while he has primarily been affected by a Neoplatonic philosophical theology and its modern parallels, I have been primarily affected by modern "idealism," an idealism that in our time can only be known as a dark or negative idealism, and most clearly negative in its inevitable enactment of the death of God, an enactment already beginning philosophically with Spinoza, and occurring in our own time in Heidegger; and while many theologians have been far more deeply affected by Heidegger than I have been, I think it of the utmost importance to understand his thinking as a culmination of our philosophical tradition, just as late modern poetry is a culmination of our poetic tradition. Perhaps only a Blakean can understand Kafka as a culmination of a uniquely Western poetic tradition, and if we can understand this tradition as beginning with Homer, and thereby beginning with the ending of an archaic or primordial night, Kafka even as Joyce certainly resurrects that night, but now darkness is total as it never was in the primordial world, and if theologically we can understand an archaic or primordial world as being innocent of "God," no such innocence is present in either Joyce or Kafka, but it is Kafka who most purely and most decisively enacts the ending of every possible innocence.

Faith itself realizes a wholly new meaning in the perspective of Kafka's writing. Here vanishes any possible "atheism," and any possible innocence of "God." Now God is overwhelmingly real, but real only as the deepest and purest darkness. Yet this is a darkness that speaks or unveils itself in the luminous clarity of Kafka's prose, a truly poetic prose in its very immediacy, and a prose that speaks us by speaking our darkness, a deep darkness that is here simply undeniable, and undeniable insofar as we can read or speak. Is this a condition transcending any possible faith, or a condition indistinguishable from faith itself, a condition immediately knowing God, and so purely so that here an unawareness of God or an unknowing of God is simply impossible? The impact of Kafka's writing has become overwhelming, and even so for the theologian, but can the theologian know this as a genuine knowledge of God, and a genuine knowledge of God for us? Twentieth-century dialectical theology could know such an understanding of God, one that Barth could decisively draw forth as the "God of religion," but this is the God who is the very opposite of the God of faith, a faith that is born by way of a genuine negation of the God of religion. This is an understanding that deeply affected my generation of theologians, but it is one that could not be sustained, first largely disappearing in Barth's dogmatic theology, and then wholly disappearing in all subsequent systematic theology, for this is a dialectical theology whose negative movement is far more powerful than its positive counterpart, thereby not only making impossible any genuine *coincidentia oppositorum*, but also making impossible any positive expression of faith with even a residue of the power of its dialectical counterpart.

One real problem with such a dialectical theology is that at its very core it is more dualistic than dialectical, so that religion and faith inevitably become dualistically rather than dialectically related, and just as this demands a purely nonhistorical understanding of religion, it also demands a finally nonhistorical understanding of faith; and while originally New Testament scholars could be deeply drawn to dialectical theology, with the passage of time this attachment withered away, although in my judgment Bultmann's *Theology of the New Testament* is the greatest achievement of dialectical theology since its inauguration in Barth's *The Epistle to the Romans*. So it is that in our time genuine biblical scholarship has become deeply atheological, with the consequence that our understanding of faith has become even more deeply ahistorical, and if only by this means deeply removed from our own situation and condition, and just thereby fully removed from any genuine meaning for us.

I had long been fascinated by literature and theology. The problem is that this has never become a genuine discipline, or not in theological circles. Along with David Jasper the one real exception to this is Robert Detweiler, whom I like to think succeeded me at Emory, and who was fully embarked upon a unique theological vocation until this was shattered by a massive stroke. Shortly before this I had seen Bob at a literature and theology conference at the University of Glasgow. He was in splendid shape, as healthy and vigorous as any theologian whom I have known, and despite his vocation, which has taken him into very dark centers and voices, he is a man of deep joy which he immediately communicates to others. Now he had suffered a catastrophic fall which is unique in the theological world, and despite the apparently wholly negative medical prognosis of a team of specialists at Emory, whom I gather were amazed that he survived at all, Bob remains very much alive, although crippled and with only a fraction of his former energy, and only by way of a continual passage through pain and suffering demanding the deepest possible discipline and sacrifice. Along with many others, I look upon Bob's present condition as a theological paradigm for us, and if here darkness and chaos are truly literal in their embodiment, it is chaos and darkness that Bob had freely chosen to explore, and just as Bob has had a deep affect upon a large number of students and associates, I expect this impact to deepen in the future, for it is my hope that he will yet give us a truly dialectical theology, and one only possible by way of a genuine embodiment of darkness.

If only through Detweiler's fall, we can sense the true dangers of every vicarious theology, of every attempt to know darkness only vicariously, or only all too indirectly. Such theology can be known as a product of what Bonhoeffer named as "cheap grace," a cheap grace which is the very opposite of grace itself, and yet a grace which Bonhoeffer could know as dominating the theological world. Of course, nowhere is such a world more comprehensive than it is in our academic world, and if here everything whatsoever is finally vicarious, or is so outside of the hard sciences themselves, this is a world that has no doubt deeply damaged theology, if it has not made theology impossible altogether, and done so if only because "experience" itself is so alien to the academic life, as perhaps best captured in the phenomenological method of reduction or *epoche*, which completely bars one from using any judgment that concerns spatial-temporal existence itself. Of course, this is far from the way of our great theologians, and even far from the way of our major twentieth-century theologians, but all such theology is now truly questionable if not simply anachronistic, for if there is one world that is truly and wholly an atheological world it is the world of postmodernity itself. Theologians of my generation were struggling with this problem even as we began our theological work, but in one sense we were deeply fortunate, for theology was then only beginning to enter the American academic world, so that if our horizon was all too limited, it was nonetheless relatively clear.

A genuine question for us is the very identity of a genuinely theological voyage. Who is it that embarks upon this voyage, what is the voyage itself, and does it have a true goal? Once again Barth became a paradigm for many if not most of us, and did so in his movement from a dialectical theology to a church dogmatics. I saw this not only as a deep disruption but also as one demonstrating the necessity of a truly solitary voyage for us, a voyage wholly unsustained by any possible corporate or institutional community, and one demanding a truly individual way. America is an apt site for such a voyage, one not only epically enacted in *Moby-Dick*, but comprehensively called forth in a uniquely American poetry, a poetry again and again enacting deep and solitary voyages, and voyages which can be understood as theological voyages, voyages into the deep, indeed, but only insofar as they are solitary voyages, and voyages liberated from every other horizon. Certainly such a voyage is a voyage into darkness, and into the depths of darkness, and if darkness can here be named as an absolute nothingness, the theologian must know that darkness as Godhead itself, and not a Godhead whose darkness is only the consequence of an epiphany of an absolute glory to us, but far rather a darkness which is Godhead itself, and is Godhead itself in the depths of its absolutely negative abyss.

That abyss has been called forth again and again at decisive points in our history, but never so comprehensively as in full modernity, and if this is now the arena in which fundamental theological work must be done, such work cannot be accomplished apart from deep risk. Here a vicarious risk is no risk at all, for inevitably genuine wounding occurs in every such venture, a wounding which I have long thought of as simply being inseparable from true theological work. Needless to say, there is a real danger here of confusing one's own sickness and weakness with such wounding, but just as we have learned that a deep anxiety is a deep *Angst*, a deep wounding transcends any possible neurosis, and even if we cannot clearly distinguish such wounding from psychosis, we can know it as issuing from our deepest depths, and those are the very depths which the theologian is called upon to name. Yes, theology is a naming of darkness, and the deeper the darkness the deeper the naming that can occur, hence I have long been hypnotized by Blake's naming of God as Satan, one which I believe made possible a revolutionary transformation of his vision, and only as a consequence of this transformation was Blake able to envision the apocalyptic Christ and apocalypse itself. But how was it possible for Blake to name God as Satan, that very Blake who gave us a more comprehensive vision of Satan than any other seer, and who could know our own selfhood as an embodiment of Satan? Is this because Blake was the first seer to envision the death of God, and because it is the dead body of God which Blake most deeply knew as Satan, a totally repressed and alienated body, and yet a body which is the body of a wholly fallen totality?

Yes, Blake has been my deepest theological model, although I have continually wondered if Blake could possibly be a genuine theological model. Indeed, Blake's vision is more deeply complex and genuinely contradictory than any other Western vision, being rivaled here only by Vajrayana Buddhism, yet Blake has had an enormous impact upon the late modern imagination, whether directly or indirectly, and it is only Blake who has given us a full vision of God as Satan, unless this is reenacted and made yet more comprehensive in *Finnegans Wake*. Why follow such a way? Certainly this is a way of knowing the deep darkness and the ultimately negative abyss of the Godhead, one which has never entered any of our theologies, and thereby it is a way of entering the absolute nothingness and the absolute nihilism of our world, and entering it through a Christian even if radical vision, for Blake was the first Western seer to envision an absolute nothingness, or to envision an absolute nothingness as absolute totality. Blake could be known as a madman even to many of his friends, and until a century after his death in 1827 literary criticism commonly judged his work to be a consequence of madness, yet such madness can be known as a holy madness, and one which is the inevitable consequence of a deeply prophetic vocation.

Theology has always resisted the contemporary prophecy which it has confronted, and the deeper the prophecy the deeper the theological resistance. Unquestionably Blake's prophetic vision is very deep, indeed, and even if it is ignored by virtually all of our theologies, thereby, too, is ignored the possibility of confronting the depths of our world, and yet ironically Blake's vision is more manifestly Christian than any other fully modern vision, leading one to wonder if it is the depths of Christianity which theology most deeply resists and opposes. There are wise ones among us who are persuaded of this, and this can occasion a genuine opposition to theology, and one even found among theologians themselves. No doubt I am one of these, nevertheless I remain a theologian, but only insofar as a profound transformation of theology is actually possible. Yet such a transformation cannot occur if faith itself is known as wholly given and unchanging, just as it is not possible unless even the deepest authority can be truly challenged; hence authority itself is inevitably a fundamental problem for the theologian, and ultimately the authority that must be most challenged theologically is the authority of God. In a real sense, every deep prophet has done this, certainly challenging everything that can be known in his or her world as the authority of God, and even when the prophet claims a higher authority of God, that is inevitably a profound challenge to every manifest authority of God.

Here, the Christian theologian faces a unique problem, and that is the problem of knowing or even naming that God who is the God of the movements of incarnation, crucifixion, and apocalypse. Milton, in his great theological treatise, *De Doctrina Christiana*, is the theologian who has here most affected me, and this occurs in his affirmation that the infinite essence or substance of God could not become incarnate, just as the supreme God could not empty Himself, for it is impossible that the very essence of God could be emptied. The truth is that this ultimate problem was not conceptually broached until Hegel, just as it was not fully imaginatively resolved until Blake, but then we truly become aware that it is the very essence of God which is "emptied" and becomes incarnate, and only this ultimately kenotic movement of self-emptying makes possible apocalypse itself, and above all so if true apocalypse is wholly other than a primordial totality or a primordial Godhead. Hence it is Godhead itself that is ultimately and profoundly transformed in these movements, a transformation that can be understood as an absolute transfiguration, an absolute transfiguration of the Godhead truly and finally shattering or reversing everything whatsoever which is given us as Godhead itself. But how is it possible to understand such a transfiguration theologically? Certainly this cannot occur apart from a total challenge to everything that we can know as theological authority, but is it possible to challenge the deepest theological authority, and the most ultimate authority of God?

This challenge surely occurs in a uniquely modern blasphemy, one most forcefully occurring in Blake, Nietzsche, and Joyce, and if the identification of God as Satan is the ultimate blasphemy, this is one that is virtually unheard in our theologies. I well remember an exciting theological colloquium on Lonergan's theology in which I participated almost thirty years ago. This was the first time that I had engaged in deep conversations with Catholic theologians, and at that time younger Lonerganians were rebelling against Lonergan's orthodoxy, and above all against his orthodox understanding of God. My paper was on the Satanic identity of Lonergan's God, and while so far as I know it was positively received, when a three-volume edition was published of the conference papers mine was the only one which was omitted. This may well have occurred to protect me, for I have never known anything but kindness and support from Catholic theologians, and in my experience the rigid orthodoxy of the dominant Protestant theological world is wholly absent in contemporary Catholic theology. Nevertheless I do not think that the Catholic theologian is open to blasphemy, and this despite the fact that many of them are deep lovers of Joyce. But was not blasphemy the primary charge against Jesus? Dante himself could identify the Papacy with the Antichrist (*Inferno* XIX, 53), and here, too, there is a deep continuity between Dante and Joyce, and if Catholic theology continues to resist the radical Catholic tradition, is there no possibility whatsoever of a genuinely radical Christian theology?

Yet this is also to ask if there is no real possibility of a genuinely radical faith. Very few real theologians would accept such an impossibility, but then only a few theologians have explored the possibility of a radical faith, and while I do not doubt that this has indeed occurred silently and privately, the published results are all too meager, and this despite the absence of theological censorship, although that is now again occurring in the Catholic world. I know of no more radical conception of faith than that which is comprehensively embodied in D. G. Leahy's *Foundation*, but there has been virtually no theological response to this, and as I discovered, it is almost impossible to find a theologian who would even review the book. Why such deep silence? Why is it now so difficult to raise the question of radical faith? Surely nothing else has so deeply banished theology from the academic world, or so alienated it from the world of biblical scholarship, or so isolated it from the great body of humanity, and yet our theologians continue to refuse to speak of radical faith. Is this now far more difficult than it was in any previous theological world, and is this because we are truly being consumed by nihilism, so that now any radical language about faith will inevitably be realized in a truly nihilistic language, and thus would necessarily be the very opposite of faith?

I must confess that I respect this position, and suspect that it is widespread among theologians today, but it has devastating consequences, of course, and is now virtually confining theology itself to our most conservative and reactionary forces. If only through Heidegger, we can know that nihilism is an ultimate question for us, and yet it is extraordinarily difficult to understand nihilism, and there is certainly no common understanding of nihilism at hand. Our clearest and deepest nihilistic philosopher, Nietzsche, devoted his final years of creativity to an ultimate attempt to conquer nihilism, and if this shattered Nietzsche himself, is this simply an impossible project? Or is radical faith itself inevitably nihilistic? It certainly is deeply antinomian, profoundly opposed to all law and authority in its own world, and this occurs in Christianity as early as Paul if not in Jesus himself, and if historical Christianity has truly and comprehensively reversed its original ground, is it possible that only the deepest nihilism could recover this ground? Already Kierkegaard could know the necessity for faith of negating historical Christianity, and it is not impossible to understand Kierkegaard as a nihilist, just as it is fully possible to understand Blake as a nihilist, and even as the Western mind almost inevitably understands Buddhism as an absolute nihilism, could this be said of the depths of faith itself? Once again Buddhism may well be a decisive theological key for us, and if it is only Buddhism that has fully known an absolute nothingness, is anything comparable to this nothingness truly incarnate in our world today?

At least from a Western point of view, Buddhism can be understood to embody an absolute transfiguration of an absolute nothingness, or an absolute transfiguration of samsara into nirvana, and something fully comparable to this does occur in a uniquely modern vision, as most clearly manifest in Nietzsche and Blake, but theologically this must finally be understood as a transfiguration of Godhead itself. Yet is this actually possible? Is it even possible to understand any kind of transfiguration of the Godhead, or does this occur in Luther's understanding of justification itself, a justification ultimately demanding a transfiguration of the God of judgment into the God of grace, and is that understanding already present in Paul, and one which has been a deep underground of Christianity throughout its history? Certainly it is not possible to think such a transfiguration apart from defying the deepest theological authority. This occurs in both Paul and Luther, of course, but must it occur in every genuine theological thinking? Paul, too, is often understood as a nihilist, and not unjustifiably, so that we must ask if it is possible to think an absolute transfiguration without thinking nihilistically, or without wholly transforming if not shattering our deepest theological categories. A deeper nihilism is not simply a negation of thinking, it is an absolute transformation of thinking, and just as many of our scholars understand Hegel as a nihilistic thinker, it is possible to understand a Hegelian *Aufhebung* as a nihilistic negation of thinking which nevertheless and precisely thereby realizes an absolute transformation of thinking itself.

Nietzsche could understand the theologian as inevitably being a nihilist, a nihilism inseparable from an affirmation of the Christian God, that God whom Nietzsche knew as being absolute No-saying and absolute No-saying alone. Here Christianity itself can be known as a pure nihilism, as an absolute assault upon life itself, and as the deepest historical source of *ressentiment*. Yet Nietzsche himself was at bottom a theologian, and surely a theologian in his ultimate project of transforming an absolute No-saying into an absolute Yes-saying, a project impossible apart from the deepest realization of No-saying, and a project impossible apart from the deepest realization of transfiguration itself. Is that project inevitably one of understanding an absolute transfiguration of Godhead itself? And is that the inevitable core of deep or genuine theological thinking today? If so, that could account for the seeming impossibility of contemporary theological thinking, but it could also establish the possibility that ours is indeed a time of profound theological transformation, one deeply preparing even if all too silently for an ultimate break which could be an ultimate breakthrough, and a breakthrough into an understanding of that Godhead which is an absolute nothingness, but is an absolute nothingness only in wholly realizing an absolute transfiguration of itself.

An absolute transfiguration is only actually possible by way of a transfiguration of absolutely opposite poles or polarities, only when these opposites are fully and actually real could this transfiguration occur. These are the full opposites which pass into each other in an absolute transfiguration, and all deep and genuine dialectical thinking and vision incorporates such a transfiguration. Twentieth-century dialectical theology was stillborn if only because it did not incorporate a fully dialectical transfiguration. Here Godhead itself is nondialectical, and therefore cannot be transfigured. This is true of virtually all theology, and certainly of all orthodox or ecclesiastical theology, with the great exception of Barth's truly dialectical understanding of election or predestination. Only in the course of many years of theological struggle was I able to open myself to the possibility of the absolute transfiguration of the Godhead, for this is only possible if the negative pole or polarity of the Godhead is absolutely real. That could only mean that Godhead itself is absolutely "evil" even as it is absolutely "good," only the deep darkness and abyss of the Godhead makes possible an absolute transfiguration. Not only is that abyss transfigured in this transfiguration, but it can even be understood that the final expression of this process could only be actually manifest in its most abysmal or negative mode. Thereby we can understand how both ancient and modern apocalypticism can know a totality of darkness, a darkness inseparable from a full and actual apocalyptic dawning, or inseparable from apocalypse itself.

So it is that we can also understand a uniquely modern absolute nothingness as such a darkness, but so, too, can we thereby understand that if an absolute transfiguration of the Godhead even now is occurring, then it could only be manifest to us in an ultimately abysmal and negative mode, so that the very advent of an absolute nothingness can be understood as an inevitable consequence of a final or ultimate transfiguration of the Godhead, and the very absence of such a nothingness could be interpreted as the absence of absolute transfiguration itself. We cannot deny that our deepest modern visionaries have entered an absolute nothingness with an ultimate affirmation, and even when this is profoundly resisted, as in Kafka, it nevertheless occurs, and inevitably occurs in the fullness of vision, a vision whose very actuality is a profound witness to the positive power of an absolute nothingness, a positive power which could be known theologically as a decisive sign of the transfiguration of Godhead itself. The very naming of absolute darkness is surely such a sign, a naming which is as deep and comprehensive as any naming that has ever occurred, and one in genuine continuity with all full apocalypticism, but one in profound discontinuity with every Gnostic dualism, or every possible dualism whatsoever.

As my theological work approaches its culmination, I can see that the transfiguration of the Godhead has become its deepest center, and if its previous center was a *coincidentia oppositorum* of Christ and Satan, that, too, can be understood as a transfiguration of the Godhead. So perhaps this has always been the deep center of my work, and while this only all too gradually became manifest, and has been hidden and obscured by conflicting turns and moves, perhaps these were necessary to this theological voyage, and necessary if only because of the weakness of this voyager. Certainly this has been a genuine voyage for me, whether pathological or not, and so, too, it has been a genuine theological voyage, whether illusory or not. For a theological voyage is truly a voyage, one realizing whatever depths are possible for us, and one occurring not in heaven or in a dreamy world of innocence, but in the very actualities of our time and world. I deeply believe that each and every one of us is called to a theological voyage, and that it inevitably occurs whether or not we are aware of it, so that in this sense theology is our most universal way, and even if theology has never been so invisible as it is today, that invisibility could be a necessary mask for its contemporary actuality, and my gravest fear about my own work is that it is an irresponsible dislodging of that mask, and one only unveiling a hollow and artificial theology. Perhaps any such unveiling will inevitably suffer this consequence, or any unveiling of our lesser voyages, but even those voyages challenge that deep silence that reigns among us, and while many can know silence as a deep theological virtue, it can no less so be an ultimate theological veil and curse.

CHAPTER 13

Apocalypse

That blessed moment finally came when I could retire from the academic world, and feeling as though I was becoming purged of a true pollution, I sought a haven in the mountains, but having become alienated from a new South, and not being able to surrender Manhattan, I sought and found a home in the Pocono Mountains. Here David Leahy has a summer home which has become a permanent home, but otherwise I knew no one whatsoever, so that now living apart from virtually any social world, I intended a deeper fulfillment of my all too solitary theological vocation. My project was a book on Godhead and the Nothing, and not Godhead and the apophatic or purely mystical Nothing, but rather Godhead and a purely negative or purely nihilistic Nothing, or that very revolutionary Nothing which is so deeply embodied in our world. That book has now been published as *Godhead and the Nothing* (SUNY Press, 2003), and so far as I know it is the only book actually investigating absolute evil, and the absolute evil of the Godhead, an absolutely negative abyss which is an inevitable consequence of an ultimate realization of the death of God, yet a fully actual absolute nothingness which is essential to the apocalyptic transfiguration of the Godhead. Of course, I had been drawn to what can be understood as a nihilistic theology from the very beginning of my work, and had long believed that a pure nihilism is the inevitable consequence of the death of God, a nihilism which now and for the first time is the very arena of all genuine theological voyages, just as it has become the arena of all our deeper imaginative and conceptual voyages. This is indeed a common judgment in our time. I share it with a significant number of theologians,

171

and I am far from being alone in being persuaded that it is a profound reaction against such nihilism that is a fundamental ground of a new fundamentalism and a new conservative or reactionary theology, one now dominating our religious and theological worlds, just as it is also true that nihilism is an impelling force in creating that new social and political conservatism which so dominates our world.

Now just as a new nihilism has been understood as a historical consequence of the French Revolution, or even of the English Revolution, nihilism can be understood as an inevitable consequence of all deep revolution. It has certainly accompanied the genuine revolutions of the modern world, and if the twentieth century is the most revolutionary age in world history, it also can be understood and even thereby as a nihilistic era, as fully manifest in its unique totalitarianisms, and nowhere is nihilism so decisively manifest as it is in our counterrevolutions, so that virtually everyone can understand Nazism as a pure nihilism. Bergman has long been my favorite film director, and he has given us our most purely nihilistic films, but also and perhaps even thereby our most purely religious films, and above all so in his great trilogy, *Winter Light*, *Through a Glass Darkly* and *The Silence,* which can be understood as giving us our purest contemporary epiphany of God. Yet all of our deeper films are in some genuine sense nihilistic. Thereby, however, they are inseparably related to our most popular movies, as our pure entertainment is inevitably nihilistic in its impact, as is fully manifest in our postmodern era, an era that it is impossible to understand without understanding nihilism. All of us are living in a nihilistic world, whether we are aware of it or not, and if we are now living in the most prosperous economic era in Western history, this is nevertheless a deeply empty and vacuous era, as depth of any kind has seemingly vanished, thereby collapsing every real distinction between appearance and reality, or the virtual and the real, or the public and the individual, or the interior and the exterior, or truth and falsehood, or good and evil.

Not only is this a nihilistic condition, but it also can be understood as an apocalyptic condition, and it cannot be denied that modern nihilism and modern apocalypticism are truly and integrally related to each other. Neither has fully been manifest or real apart from the other, and just as our deepest revolutionary thinkers have been apocalyptic thinkers, all of our genuine modern revolutions have been manifestly and overtly apocalyptic, even including the scientific revolution of the seventeenth century, which certainly brought to an end an old world and inaugurated a truly and even absolutely new world. But as Nietzsche declared, ever since Copernicus humanity has been falling into a "mysterious X," a truly new vacuity or void, one which Nietzsche knew as a new and absolute nihilism, but nevertheless an apocalyptic nihilism, apocalyptic in the totality of its negation of an old world, and apocalyptic in its unveiling of the totality of a new incarnate darkness, a darkness which alone is the site of true apocalyptic dawning, a dawning which Nietzsche could know as the advent of "Zarathustra" or of an absolutely new Eternal Recurrence. Clearly, apocalypticism is nihilistic in the totality of its movement of negation, and clearly nihilism is apocalyptic in its ending of an old world. All of our nihilistic movements have been apocalyptic in a genuine sense, even including Nazism, so that a pure nihilism can be understood as an apocalyptic nihilism, thus raising the question of how it is possible to distinguish nihilism and apocalypticism.

Both nihilism and apocalypticism are deeply antinomian, truly and even absolutely assaulting all established or given law and authority, so that conservative thinkers can responsibly know modern apocalypticism as a modern nihilism. Hence the birth of modern nihilism can be known as occurring in the French Revolution, a truly apocalyptic revolution, as first unveiled by Hegel himself. Yet the very birth of modernity is indistinguishable from the ending of the ancient and primordial movement of eternal return. With this ending it becomes overwhelmingly manifest and real that there is no possibility whatsoever of a return to an earlier historical time, hence no possibility at all of returning to a premodern world, and therefore no possibility of returning to a pre-nihilistic world. Is the advent of a nihilistic world the advent of a new and absolutely apocalyptic world, or the advent of an essential condition for the dawning of an absolutely new apocalypse, a condition apart from which no such apocalypse is possible? Have we now indeed truly entered that apocalypse, and despite the darkness of our world is that world finally an apocalyptic world, and an apocalyptic world which has already and finally dawned? Blake, Hegel, and Nietzsche genuinely and profoundly enacted such an apocalyptic advent, thereby renewing the apocalyptic enactments of Jesus and Paul, but has such an enactment now become realized in our most public and common and universal worlds?

In my judgment, D. G. Leahy is now our most profound and original thinker, and he is a truly and purely apocalyptic thinker, not only
calling forth the totality of the *novitas mundi*, but purely thinking that
totality in what he continually names as the "thinking now occurring
for the first time," as now thinking itself is and only can be a purely
apocalyptic thinking. Once I moved to the Poconos, I saw even more
of David, and I shall never forget his deep affirmations that the world
has now actually come to an end, and that even now we are living in
an absolutely new apocalypse. Such an affirmation is not new for a
Christian thinker—one has only to think of a Paul or a Hegel—and as
I had discovered this affirmation and enactment consistently and continually occurs throughout the Christian epic tradition from Dante
through Joyce. But now this affirmation is open for everyone, and is
even enacted in our actual acts, or in those acts which are actual in this
new world. Now this situation is very odd indeed, for nothing is seemingly more absurd or illusory than a genuine apocalypticism. Nothing
more violates common sense than an affirmation that the world has
already come to an end, yet such an affirmation truly resonates in our
world, and perhaps far more so than in any previous historical world.
It is as though it were simply a statement of what at bottom is true, or
is even undeniable, or undeniable to those who are awake.

A genuine paradox is manifest in all deeply and ultimately religious movements, and that is that the deepest depths of our religious
or sacred enactments are ultimately identical with our most common
and actual enactments, so that truly sacred language is finally a truly
common language, as fully manifest not only in the parables of Jesus
but also in Zen or Chan Buddhism, and as drawn forth so purely for us
by Wittgenstein, who was surely deeply betrayed by an analytic philosophy that could know a common language as simply and only a
common language. Perhaps film is that twentieth-century art which
most openly captures this identity, and if film is that post-primordial
or post-archaic art which truly is an art for everyone, we certainly
have been given truly sacred films, but it is all too significant that virtually all of these have vanished from the mass market, and so far as I
know no book has yet been written on this important subject. Is our
deepest religious or sacred life truly invisible to us? Perhaps it is
embodied in architecture, which is surely true in the sacred architecture of the past, but if so it is invisible to us. Mark Taylor in *Disfigur-*

ing has explored the sacred dimension of both modern and postmodern architecture, yet this has had little if any effect upon our theological understanding. Taylor and many others would now have us believe that theological understanding itself has become anachronistic. If so, it thereby joins all metaphysical understanding, or all deeper conceptual understanding, or even everything that was once manifest as understanding in all previous worlds.

This, too, is both a nihilistic and an apocalyptic condition, but can it be understood by everyone, or by everyone to whom it is evoked? Can one understand it simply by becoming open to the actualities of our contemporary world? Is it possible to understand Leahy as the Hegel of our time and world? His language is certainly more deeply abstract than any other contemporary language, and, like Hegel's, his is a genuinely apocalyptic language, and again like Hegel's one truly reflecting his own historical world. Of course, for both that world is finally the world of the future, and of an apocalyptic future. Yet that future has already dawned, and is even now our deepest reality, a reality that is truly universal, and is fully manifest wherever consciousness or thinking are actual and real. Hence this is an apocalypse that truly is known by everyone, and even if this is a knowledge lying beyond or beneath our apparent or manifest knowledge, it is nonetheless real, so that we truly respond to it whenever we confront it, and then it becomes undeniably real for us. One of the remarkable qualities about Leahy is the power of his voice. As Ray Hart observed, one can understand and respond to his speech even when one cannot understand his writing, and as I discovered on very different occasions, Leahy can speak so as to be understood by virtually everyone, even if almost no one can now understand his writing.

I think that there is a genuine truth in this odd phenomenon, and that is that the deepest truth can be genuinely ultimate and openly manifest at once. A great body of Nietzsche's writing fully exhibits this, and at no other point is he more distant from a Hegel or a Heidegger. Both Christianity and Buddhism know their founders as having spoken such a language, so that a truly common language can be a truly ultimate language, and when ultimate language is actually or fully spoken it has a truly universal impact. Once I was frequently asked if it is possible to falsify the proposition that God is dead, and I often responded that if it is possible to discover a usage of the word

"God" in contemporary discourse that is truly positive or affirmative, then the proposition would be falsified. This is in large measure a rhetorical game, although it can be played very seriously with our contemporary philosophical and literary discourse, but it was intended to draw forth the ultimacy of language, and of our contemporary language, and each and every one of us can respond to this. There is a profound and final ultimacy of speech that I attempted to draw forth in *The Self-Embodiment of God*, and this is one that is open to all, so that if something cannot truly or actually be spoken, then it cannot be real, although genuine silence can be a vehicle of speech, and when speech does truly occur, then its impact is not only undeniable but truly universal in its own horizon of hearing, and at bottom such speech can be heard by everyone.

One of the truly demonic dimensions of every Gnosticism is the chasm that it establishes between the "perfect" and the common, or the elect and everyone else, and I have never encountered a genuine thinker or artist who exhibited even a trace of such a judgment. Indeed, this can even be employed as a pragmatic test in the academic world to distinguish the artificial from the genuine. Blake's "The Eternal Humanity Divine" and Joyce's "Here Comes Everybody" are both witnesses to and evocations of a universal humanity that is actuality itself, and while this is a humanity that is absolutely other than our seemingly common condition, it is in fact embodied in that condition, and we awaken our actual humanity when we encounter a fully actual or a truly actual speech. Of course, there can be demonic if not Satanic expressions of speech, but these can never occur apart from genuine laceration, lacerations manifestly occurring in the hearers of such speech, but the very opposite occurs in the realization of genuine speech, and the hearing of that speech is liberation, a liberation accompanied by true joy. The empiricist may well ask how one can distinguish genuine laceration from genuine joy, and this may well be impossible from any external perspective, but it is not impossible for one who truly hears, and we all at least potentially can truly hear, and true hearing has manifestly had a revolutionary impact upon our history.

Can we now hear an apocalyptic ending, or do we actually hear an apocalyptic ending? But this is simultaneously to ask if we hear an apocalyptic beginning, a beginning which is an absolute beginning, and the absolute beginning of absolute apocalypse itself. While this may well be a specifically or uniquely Christian question, it nevertheless has a universal resonance in our world, and just as it is possible to understand a uniquely modern apocalypticism as a transformation of an original Christian apocalypticism, it may well be possible to understand a contemporary apocalypticism as such a transformation, thus giving a contemporary ironic meaning to the ancient Christian affirmation that the "soul" is naturally Christian. Of course, Christianity became a world religion only by negating its original apocalyptic ground, but if we can understand the ending of Christendom as an apocalyptic ending, that ending could then be understood as the renewal of an original apocalyptic ending, and therewith the renewal of apocalypse itself. But can we hear apocalypse itself in our very midst? Surely we can know the advent of a dark apocalypse in our world, and know it as being embodied in a nihilistic world, but can we know that dark apocalypse as a joyous apocalypse, and one promising if not embodying an absolute transfiguration? This very question, perhaps now my primal question, takes me back to my original initiation, an initiation into the very body of Satan, but now a body of Satan that is manifestly a universal body, and one emptying everything and everyone that it enacts.

If only in this perspective, it is now far easier for me to understand my theological vocation as a surrogate for others. No doubt others have followed it far more truly than I have, but if I am alone as a theologian of Satan, I am also now apparently alone as an apocalyptic theologian, even if these very vocations now have a universal import that is truly new, perhaps now ending every other theological way, or every way that is closed to this one. Thus in the twilight of my life, I sense that I have been given an overwhelming gift. One might think of a canary in the mine in considering my theological life: so long as there is any movement at all the darkness is not yet total. This is a darkness in which genuine mining is occurring, and even if it is unheard and invisible to us, if we can name our darkness we can remain open to that mining, and this naming could be understood as the purest vocation of theology. Yes, the primary calling of the theologian is to name God, and to name that God who can actually be named by us, and if this calling has seemingly now ended, that could be because the theologian has not yet truly named our darkness, and thus not yet truly named God. While silence is now the primary path of the theologian, and above all silence about God, this is a silence which I have ever more deeply and ever more comprehensively refused, for I am simply incapable of not naming God, and perhaps most deeply because of that very initiation which I was given.

Is some such initiation essential to every theologian, or to every fundamental theologian, and is this why genuine theology simply cannot be taught academically, is now inevitably absent from our theological schools, and likewise absent from our public or our common worlds? There are those who speak of me as the last theologian, and I must confess that I sometimes think that I am now the only one writing theology. Perhaps genuine theological writing has always been a deep curse, and it certainly is a decisive way of dissolving if not reversing all innocence, and above all so in our world. If we understand Paul as our first theologian, then the thorn in his flesh could well have been theology itself, and just as I do not believe that there has ever been a genuine Christian theologian who was not a Pauline theologian, I do not believe that it is possible to be a theologian apart from a voyage into darkness, and if my theological work has been such a voyage, it was truly inaugurated by my initiation into Satan. My primary theological models have been those who have undergone such an initiation, thus I understand a theological naming of God as a naming of darkness, and if now every other naming of God has ended, our theological calling may now be purer than it has ever previously been, and even purer as a theological calling, a calling that can name and enact darkness alone, but that very naming stills the darkness, and stills it so as to make it our own.

The theologian with whom I was most allied in the theological exploration of our darkness was Charlie Winquist. Although each of us underwent enormous transformations in our theological pilgrimage, our work had always been centered upon an ultimate darkness or an ultimate void, thus it was seemingly the most negative voices in our world to which we were most drawn, with the manifest conviction that these are the voices that most call forth our ultimate condition, and our ultimate theological condition. Charlie was one of the great theological teachers of our time, and he had a deeper impact upon his students than anyone else whom I know, and despite the enormous support that they gave him, Charlie was finally alone. His work was culminating with a theology of desire, one profoundly affected by Freud, Lacan, and Kristeva, hence it is a theology of celebration, and a celebration of an absolute Joy. But this was the very time that his alcoholism was reaching its fruition, one effecting an ultimate medical crisis, and one that had no possible medical resolution. I regularly visited him in Syracuse while he was in this condition. Now genuine conversation was impossible, and Charlie himself was removed from all possible desire. We had no doubt that he knew that he was dying, and yet never then did I hear him speak a bitter word, or show even the slightest sense of *ressentiment*, and despite his dreadful condition, he apparently embodied a genuine peace and acceptance. Upon his death, I was invited to give the major address at his memorial service, a truly overwhelming challenge. Somehow I was able to write the address, but only by sensing that Charlie was alive and with us, and even speaking through me. Yes, we are celebrants of Joy, but only by being celebrants of Darkness, and if our deepest desire is for Joy, that desire can only be realized through the deepest darkness.

Finally, this is a darkness in response to which we can only say Yes, and if this is our deeper theological calling, one to which everyone is called, my way has been one of naming that darkness as God. While I believe that ultimately we can only say Yes to God, now that means saying Yes to the absolute darkness or the absolute nothingness of God, and hence saying Yes to absolute nothingness or absolute darkness itself. My physicist friends once joked with me about how naïve all philosophers of science are, how closed they are to the deep chaos of truly modern science, and modern science truly has said Yes to an ultimate chaos. Thereby it can be understood to be truly Faustian, but it embraces that absolute No so as to transfigure it into an absolute Yes, and just as my one published article on science is entitled "Satan as the Messiah of Nature," genuine science can be understood as a transfiguration of nature, and if only in this sense, it can thereby be understood as a consequence of Christianity. The Faust myth is perhaps the one truly unique modern Western myth, and whether or not modern science truly can be understood as Faustian, truly modern theology certainly can, and above all a uniquely modern theology, a theology knowing and enacting an absolute No, an absolute No apart from which there cannot possibly be an absolute Yes. Yet truly to know that No is finally to know that Yes!

Hence the way for us is inevitably the way down. Certainly this has been my own theological path, and I believe that ultimately it is shared by us all.

My one great lament about my own work is that it did not dare to become open to the deepest and most absolute No. This I had hoped to rectify in my retirement, for this way demands genuine solitude, and genuine isolation as well. My retirement has given me this, but there is certainly every probability that I will not fully prosecute this calling, in which case I will finally be a theological failure, and I cannot dissociate true theological failure from damnation itself. Once again I ask how one could be a true theologian without a genuine sense of damnation. By this criterion I surely am a theologian, but inasmuch as I believe that this is a universal condition, all of us finally are theologians, and theologians precisely in thinking about our damnation. So it is that late modernity is a truly theological age, perhaps more deeply so than any previous age, and if thereby theology is truly disguised, that disguise is dislodged in our darkest moments, then we do think damnation, and damnation is our deepest contemporary theological category, our most actual theological name. Yes, the most actual name of God for us is truly the name of Satan. Each of us knows and speaks that name, and we speak it in truly or actually naming our darkness. Hence all of us know God, or know God insofar as we can name our deepest darkness. Yes, the world is ultimately dark today, a darkness inseparable from its very emptiness, but in naming that emptiness we become open to its possible transfiguration, and the ultimate actuality of this emptiness cannot finally be dissociated from the possibility if not the actuality of its ultimate transfiguration.

Yes, the darkness is deepest immediately prior to any possible dawn, but then that darkness can be known as light itself, a darkness inseparable from the advent of light, so that in naming that darkness we do name the light, just as in truly naming the darkness of God we precisely thereby name an ultimate transfiguration. This has manifestly occurred in our deeper art and poetry, so that we cannot fully be open to the depths of the imagination without being open to the depths of transfiguration itself; so, too, we cannot be open to the depths of the darkness of God apart from being open to an absolute apocalypse, an absolute apocalypse which is an absolute transfiguration, and an absolute transfiguration of the depths of darkness itself. Yes, our soul is "naturally" Christian, but only insofar as it is naturally dark. Theologically, our task is to name that darkness, not that I have yet succeeded in truly doing this, but if old age is an age of darkness, I may yet fully become a theologian, and if now theology is impossible for the young, this may well be because theology is now inevitable for the truly old. It is often said that death is unreal for the truly young, although I have never believed this, for I have known death throughout my life, a knowledge apart from which I could never have become a theologian.

Nietzsche could know Christianity as the one absolute curse in our history and world. Now theology itself can be known as such a curse, and if this is true it could only thrive in our darkness, and perhaps it is now far more universally present than we can know. I must confess that I tend to see it everywhere, and to see it everywhere where darkness is truly and actually present. Yet the actual presence of darkness is truly different from any possible actual totality of darkness. Such a totality could not possibly be named, or could be named only by way of a total silence, so that in actually naming our darkness we are inevitably open to its very opposite, so that we cannot truly name darkness apart from joy. This is a joy which I have certainly known theologically, and a joy which I spoke insofar as I could preach, and if all of my genuine theological writing is preaching itself, I can relish an image of myself as a Southern preacher, and perhaps I am the last truly Southern preacher, and if only thereby the last theologian. Southern literature now appears to be dead, or dead in its deeper expressions, so perhaps I am already dead, and dead above all as a theologian. My theological writing could now simply be the recoil of a recent corpse, but if so I hope that I have died with my boots on, my theological boots, and that these boots could be a useful artifact for future theologians, archeological witnesses to the presence of theology in our desert, for perhaps theology is that one curse than can never finally disappear.

Must we inevitably die as hollow men or women? Rilke could declare that our only real fear of death is to die with unlived life in our bodies, and perhaps our only real terror of death is to die with our theological voyage unfulfilled or abated, and if finally there is but one sorrow and that is not to be a saint, that is the sorrow of damnation itself, and I shall never forget John Bunyan's belief that the only certain sign of a damned soul is a peaceful and happy death. Is our "day" finally only a long day's journey into the night, and is this that archetypal story or plot which finally underlies every actual story, and does so even in a postmodern disavowal of every master plot or key, a disavowal that can disenact every story but this one? For our death is an absolutely inevitable destiny, and finally death itself is the center of every theology, a death wholly transcending any possible decentering, or any possible reversal. Many theologians can know immortality as the deepest possible pagan belief, as the very refusal of grace itself, but ours is a world in which immortality can no longer actually be thought or actually imagined, and is seemingly possible only by way of passivity or withdrawal, a withdrawal and passivity that can be known as death itself, and even if images of death are our most forbidden images, they are precisely thereby our most hypnotizing and compulsive images, and those very images by which we are most immediately awakened.

If our awakening is then an awakening to death, it is our own death which occasions such awakening, a death which is our own and not another's, but this death is inseparable from a theological voyage, a theological voyage which calls each and every one of us, and does so with an irresistible finality. While Spinoza could foreswear all meditation upon death, is that an actual possibility for us? Is meditation inevitably a meditation upon death and precisely thereby a liberating meditation, an enactment of death itself in our truest center, and is it only thereby that this center is finally real? If this is our ultimate meditation, it is just thereby a theological meditation, and if theological meditation for us is inevitably a meditation upon God, this could only be for us a meditation upon the death of God, for a meditation calling forth the ultimacy of death can only culminate in a meditation upon the death of God. That meditation occurs in every genuine meditation upon the Crucifixion, but the deepest meditation upon death can be understood as meditation upon crucifixion. Here Christianity and Buddhism are truly parallel to each other, but every deep meditation upon death is a meditation upon the ultimacy and finality of death, and nowhere is that finality and ultimacy more fully called forth symbolically than it is in the very symbol of crucifixion. Now if it is only in our own time that the ultimacy and finality of death have become truly universal, thereby dissolving every genuine image and symbol of immortality, it is perhaps only in our time that meditation upon the finality of death has become comprehensively universal, occurring wherever life is actual and real.

This alone could illuminate the deep interior desert of our world, one accompanied by a dazzling and wholly empty exteriority, but thereby we can know our actual condition as a genuine coffin. A coffin, it is true, generating illusions of light, which seemingly are more pervasive now than ever previously in our history, but their very emptiness is a decisive sign of that coffin which is their source, and a coffin that is called forth whenever we can actually see or speak. So it is that theology is now inevitably a coffin theology or a theology of death, and if the very aura of death is the most distinctive sign or mark of theology itself, theology could be far more pervasive today than we can imagine, and just as the ancient world did not become a fully theological world until the classical world had ended, our world in its very death throes may well be undergoing a full theological epiphany, and even as Hellenistic theology is vastly distant from all ancient Greek theology, with the possible exception of Plato, our actual theology will be vastly distant from everything that we have known as theology, with the exception of those theologies which are most deeply precursors of our condition. Yet if there is one thing that Hellenistic theology could not know, with the great exception of Augustine himself, it is a pure joy, an ultimate Yes-saying, and if Augustine could know this joy in response to the ending of the ancient world, perhaps we can know a pure joy in response to the ending of the world itself.

Such a joy must be wholly distinguished from any possible Gnostic affirmation, or from any pure dualism. Here joy could only be a total joy, a joy embracing totality itself, and hence embracing that very world which is coming to an end. All of our great artists have mediated such a joy to us, and even if great art is seemingly wholly absent from our world, this very situation could make possible a new universal joy, a truly common joy, one which a Jesus or a Gotama could already evoke. Yet an ultimate joy has been called forth in our world by our greatest modern prophets, Blake and Nietzsche, and while this is a joy that can only be evoked in the heart of darkness, and is even made possible by that very darkness, it is a joy wholly transcending every possible darkness. If that is the joy to which we are finally most deeply called, it is inseparable from the ultimate depths of darkness, and hence inseparable from an eternal death. But if that eternal death is commonly or universally embodied as it has never been before, so, too, an absolutely new and universal joy could be at hand, a joy evoked by the very symbol of apocalypse, and if ours is truly an apocalyptic age, it cannot truly be so apart from an apocalyptic joy, so that in truly naming our apocalyptic death we thereby name apocalyptic joy, thus a genuine theology of death is finally a theology of joy, but a joy only known through the ultimacy and finality of death itself, or of that death embodied in an absolute apocalypse.

Index